Minnesota Marvels

Minnesota Marvels

Roadside Attractions
in the Land of Lakes

Eric Dregni

University of Minnesota Press
Minneapolis • London

Map by Parrot Graphics

Published by the University of Minnesota Press
111 Third Avenue South, Suite 290
Minneapolis, MN 55401-2520
http://www.upress.umn.edu

Library of Congress Cataloging-in-Publication Data

Dregni, Eric, 1968–
    Minnesota marvels : roadside attractions in the Land of Lakes /
Eric Dregni.
        p.   cm.
    Includes bibliographical references (p.   ) and index.
    ISBN 0-8166-3632-X (pbk. : alk. paper)
    1. Minnesota—Guidebooks.   2. Minnesota—Description and
travel.   3. Historic sites—Minnesota—Guidebooks.   4. Roadside
architecture—Minnesota—Guidebooks.   5. Curiosities and
wonders—Minnesota—Guidebooks.   I. Title.
    F604.3 .D74 2001
    917.7604'54—dc21

                                                    2001002244

Printed in the United States of America on acid-free paper

The University of Minnesota is an equal-opportunity educator and employer.

12 11 10 09 08 07 06 05 04 03 02 01   10 9 8 7 6 5 4 3 2 1

"It's a swell state, Minnesota."

—Judy Garland

Contents

Minnesota Marvels

Akeley

Albert Lea

Alexandria

Austin

Beaver Bay

Belle Plaine

Bemidji

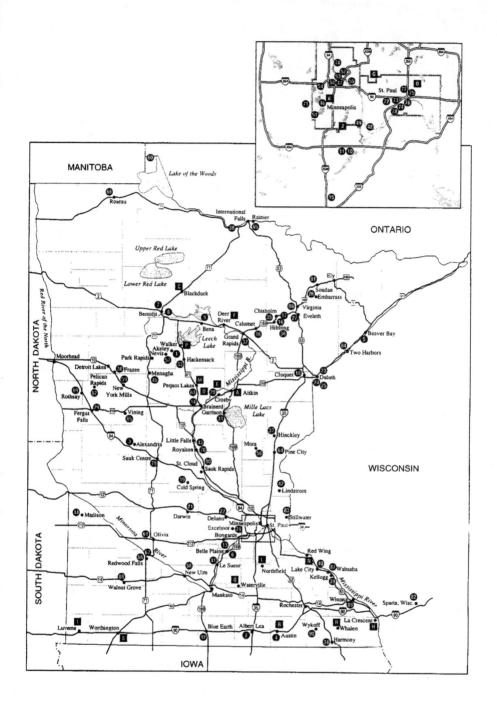

MANITOBA

Lake of the Woods

ONTARIO

Upper Red Lake

Lower Red Lake

Red River of the North

NORTH DAKOTA

International Falls
Rainier

Roseau

Blackduck

Ely
Soudan
Embarrass

Bemidji

Deer River
Chisholm
Virginia
Eveleth

Bena
Leech Lake

Calumet
Hibbing

Grand Rapids

Beaver Bay

Walker
Akeley
Nevis

Two Harbors

Hackensack

Moorhead

Park Rapids

Detroit Lakes
Frazee

Menagha

Cloquet
Duluth

Pelican Rapids
New York Mills

Pequot Lakes

Rothsay

Crosby
Aitkin

Vining

Brainerd
Garrison

Mille Lacs Lake

Fergus Falls

Mississippi R.

Alexandria

Hinckley

Little Falls
Royalton

Mora
Pine City

Sauk Centre

St. Cloud

WISCONSIN

Sauk Rapids

Cold Spring

Lindstrom

Madison

Darwin

Minnesota River

Olivia

Delano

Stillwater

Excelsior
Bongards

Minneapolis
St. Paul

Belle Plaine

Red Wing

Redwood Falls

Le Sueur

Lake City
Wabasha
Kellogg

New Ulm

Northfield

Walnut Grove

Waterville

Mississippi River

Mankato

Winona

Sparta, Wisc.

Rochester

SOUTH DAKOTA

Luverne
Worthington

Blue Earth
Albert Lea

Wykoff

La Crescent
Whalen

Austin

Harmony

IOWA

St. Paul
Minneapolis

Map of Minnesota Marvels

1. Akeley, *World's Largest Paul Bunyan*
2. Albert Lea, *Itasca Rock Garden*
3. Alexandria, *Kensington Runestone*
4. Austin, *Spam Museum*
5. Beaver Bay, *Split Rock Lighthouse State Park*
6. Belle Plaine, *Two-Story Outhouse*
7. Bemidji, *Fireplace of the States*
8. Bemidji, *Original Paul Bunyan*
9. Bena, *Big Fish Supper Club*
10. Bloomington, *Mall of America*
11. Bloomington, *Thunderbird Motel*
12. Blue Earth, *Jolly Green Giant*
13. Bongards, *Humongous Holstein*
14. Brainerd, *Paul Bunyan Amusement Center*
15. Burnsville, *Fantasuite Hotel*
16. Calumet, *Hill Annex Mine*
17. Chisholm, *Ironworld Discovery Center*
18. Cloquet, *Frank Lloyd Wright Gas Station*
19. Cold Spring, *Grasshopper Chapel*
20. Crosby, *Nordic Inn Medieval B & B*
21. Darwin, *World's Largest Ball of Twine*
22. Delano, *Blue-Eyed Chicken*
23. Duluth, *Glensheen Mansion*
24. Duluth, *William A. Irvin Steamer*
25. Duluth, *World's Largest Aerial Lift Bridge*
26. Embarrass, *The Nation's Cold Spot*
27. Eveleth, *U.S. Hockey Hall of Fame*
28. Excelsior, *Minnehaha Streetcar Boat*
29. Fergus Falls, *World's Largest Otter*
30. Frazee, *World's Largest Turkey*
31. Garrison, *Walleye Capital of the World*
32. Grand Rapids, *Judy Garland Tour*
33. Hackensack, *Home of Paul Bunyan's Sweetheart*

68. Roseau, *Polaris Snowmobile Tours*
69. Rothsay, *World's Largest Prairie Chicken*
70. Royalton, *Treasure City*
71. St. Louis Park, *Pavek's Museum of Wonderful Wireless*
72. St. Paul, *El Dorado Conquistador Collection*
73. St. Paul, *Forepaugh and Griggs Mansions*
74. St. Paul, *Gangster Tours*
75. St. Paul, *God of Peace*
76. St. Paul, *Iggy the Lizard*
77. St. Paul, *Jackson Street Railroad Roundhouse*
78. St. Paul/Minneapolis, *Schmidt and Grain Belt Breweries*
79. Sauk Centre, *Sinclair Lewis's Hometown*
80. Sauk Rapids, *Molehill Rock Garden*
81. Soudan, *Soudan Mine*
82. Sparta, Wisconsin, *F.A.S.T.*
83. Stillwater, *Vittorio's Bootlegger Caves*
84. Two Harbors, *3M/Dwan Sandpaper Museum*
85. Vining, *Small Town Sculpture Park*
86. Virginia, *World's Largest Floating Loon*
87. Wabasha, *Anderson House Hotel*
88. Walnut Grove, *Laura Ingalls Wilder Tour*
89. Winona, *Julius C. Wilkie Steamboat*
90. Wykoff, *Ed's Museum*

Events

A. Aitkin, *Fish House Parade*
B. Austin, *Spam Town, U.S.A., Festival*
C. Blackduck, *Duck Days*
D. Crosslake, *Drive-In Church*
E. Cuyuna, *Woodtick Races*
F. Deer River, *Wild Rice Festival*
G. Falcon Heights, *Minnesota State Fair*
H. La Crescent, *King Apple Grand Parade*

I. Luverne, *Buffalo Days*
J. Minneapolis, *Aquatennial Milk Carton Boat Races*
K. Minneapolis, *Art Car Parade*
L. Northfield, *Defeat of Jesse James Days*
M. Pequot Lakes, *Beanhole Days*
N. Red Wing, *Prairie Island Powwow*
O. St. Paul, *Winter Carnival*
P. Walker, *International Eelpout Festival*
Q. Waterville, *Bullhead Days*
R. Whalen, *Stand Still Parade*
S. Worthington, *Great Gobbler Gallop*

Minnesota Marvels by Region

North Central/West

Akeley, *World's Largest Paul Bunyan*

Alexandria, *Kensington Runestone*

Bemidji, *Original Paul Bunyan* and *Fireplace of the States*

Bena, *Big Fish Supper Club*

Brainerd, *Paul Bunyan Amusement Center*

Cold Spring, *Grasshopper Chapel*

Crosby, *Nordic Inn Medieval B & B*

Fergus Falls, *World's Largest Otter*

Frazee, *World's Largest Turkey*

Garrison, *Walleye Capital of the World*

Hackensack, *Home of Paul Bunyan's Sweetheart*

Little Falls, *Charles Lindbergh House*

Menagha, *Saint Urho*

Nevis, *World's Largest Tiger Muskie*

New York Mills, *Art Park and Philosophy Parade*

Northwest Angle, *Fort St. Charles*

Pelican Rapids, *World's Largest Pelican*

Pequot Lakes, *Paul Bunyan's Fishing Bobber*

Roseau, *Polaris Snowmobile Tours*

Rothsay, *World's Largest Prairie Chicken*

Royalton, *Treasure City*

Sauk Centre, *Sinclair Lewis's Hometown*

Sauk Rapids, *Molehill Rock Garden*

Vining, *Small Town Sculpture Park*

Events

Blackduck, *Duck Days*

Crosslake, *Drive-In Church*

Cuyuna, *Woodtick Races*

Pequot Lakes, *Beanhole Days*

Walker, *International Eelpout Festival*

Northeast

Beaver Bay, *Split Rock Lighthouse State Park*

Calumet, *Hill Annex Mine*

Chisholm, *Ironworld Discovery Center*

Cloquet, *Frank Lloyd Wright Gas Station*

Duluth, *Glensheen Mansion; William A. Irvin Steamer; World's Largest Aerial Lift Bridge*

Embarrass, *The Nation's Cold Spot*

Eveleth, *U.S. Hockey Hall of Fame*

Grand Rapids, *Judy Garland Tour*

Hibbing, *Greyhound Bus Origin Center* and *World's Largest Open Pit Iron Ore Mine*

Hinckley, *Fire Museum*

International Falls, *Grand Mound*

Mora, *World's Largest Dala Horse*

Pine City, *Perseverance the Voyageur*

Ranier, *Big Vic the Voyageur*

Soudan, *Soudan Mine*

Two Harbors, *3M/Dwan Sandpaper Museum*

Virginia, *World's Largest Floating Loon*

Events

Aitkin, *Fish House Parade*

Deer River, *Wild Rice Festival*

South

Albert Lea, *Itasca Rock Garden*

Austin, *Spam Museum*

Blue Earth, *Jolly Green Giant*

Darwin, *World's Largest Ball of Twine*

Delano, *Blue-Eyed Chicken*

Harmony, *Crystal Wedding Chapel*

Kellogg, *Lark Toy Museum*

Lake City, *Home of Waterskiing*

Le Sueur, *W. W. Mayo House*

Madison, *Lutefisk Capital, U.S.A.*

New Ulm, *Little Deutschland*

Olivia, *Corn Capital*

Redwood Falls, *Lower Sioux Agency Historic Site* and *Minnesota Inventors Hall of Fame*

Sparta, Wisconsin, *F.A.S.T.*

Wabasha, *Anderson House Hotel*

Walnut Grove, *Laura Ingalls Wilder Tour*

Winona, *Julius C. Wilkie Steamboat*

Wykoff, *Ed's Museum*

Events

Austin, *Spam Town, U.S.A., Festival*

La Crescent, *King Apple Grand Parade*

Luverne, *Buffalo Days*

Northfield, *Defeat of Jesse James Days*

Red Wing, *Prairie Island Powwow*

Waterville, *Bullhead Days*

Whalen, *Stand Still Parade*

Worthington, *Great Gobbler Gallop*

Twin Cities

Belle Plaine, *Two-Story Outhouse*

Bloomington, *Mall of America* and *Thunderbird Motel*

Bongards, *Humongous Holstein*

Burnsville, *Fantasuite Hotel*

Excelsior, *Minnehaha Streetcar Boat*

Lindstrom, *Little Sweden*

Minneapolis, *Bakken Library and Museum; The Band Box; Fort Snelling; Minnehaha Falls; Foshay Tower; Lake Harriet Trolley and Museum; Museum of Questionable Medical Devices; Ray Crump's Baseball Hall of Fame; Sculpture Garden and Loring Park; Weisman Art Museum*

St. Louis Park, *Pavek's Museum of Wonderful Wireless*

St. Paul, *El Dorado Conquistador Collection; Forepaugh
   and Griggs Mansions; Gangster Tours; God of Peace;
   Iggy the Lizard; Jackson Street Railroad Roundhouse*

St. Paul/Minneapolis, *Schmidt and Grain Belt Breweries*

Stillwater, *Vittorio's Bootlegger Caves*

Events

Falcon Heights, *Minnesota State Fair*

Minneapolis, *Aquatennial Milk Carton Boat Races* and
   Art Car Parade

St. Paul, *Winter Carnival*

Author's Note

These sites have been researched to the best of my ability, but some of the information about these roadside attractions may have changed since the writing or publication of this book. Sculptures may have burned (as in the case of Frazee's turkey), yet another "World's Largest" honor may have been surpassed, or an attraction (such as the Spam Museum in Austin) may have expanded to a new and improved facility. Please let me know of any changes, recommendations, or missed roadside attractions—I know there are many more fish statues out there!

Eric Dregni
P.O. Box 6381
Minneapolis, MN 55406

Acknowledgments

Sig, for confirming the Vikings' presence in Minnesota; Sonia la fotó-grafa; Guido il Postino; Michael Dapper, for Polaris leads; big bro' Michael; Jon-Jon for woodtick pointers; der 'rents, for keeping us clear of KOAs; Tim Gartman, for leading me to Vining; Professor Godollei and her car of many colors; Mary Harris at Hormel, for making clear the finer points of Spam; Nick Hook, for bringing me to Xanadu, the Foam House of Tomorrow, before its untimely demise; Kerry Keyes at the Walker; Elizabeth at the Bakken, for showing dubious electrical treatments; Leif "the reluctant Viking" Larsen; Marina "Minnesota mosquitos are like vultures!" Leonardi; Piccola Katy—the best travel-ing companion around; Rog Meyers, for his keen eye for big fish and infinite knowledge of beer; Mike Nilles, for (not) "the suckiest twenty minutes of [his] life"; Willy "Vespa King" Niskanen; Ken Nyberg; Todd Orjala at the University of Minnesota Press, for believing in the value of enormous fiberglass weirdness; Lib Peck, for an "in" to Gehry's fish; John Perkins, for theme music about bakin' bacon pies; Lance Potter at the Weisman; JP, for the big rock in Ely; Ian, for bordello-chic supper klubs; Roberto "Bob" Serio; Grandpa Cliff, for dirt on the Mayos; Andy Steiner and John Manning, for leads on stainless steel museums; Margaret Tehven and her "incorruptible"; Uncle Fun in Chicago; David Unowsky and everyone at the bookstore formerly known as Hungry Mind; Jerry Vettrus at F.A.S.T. and his splendid "graveyard"; Chris Welsch; and Pope Wentworth, for conquistador curating.

Introduction

Minnesotans are usually a soft-spoken bunch. Our state muffin is blueberry, our state fish is the tasty walleye, and our state flower is the precious showy lady slipper. We don't interrupt; we always say "please" and "thank you"; we never brag; and when we don't agree, we just smile and nod. This is called "Minnesota Nice."

The book you're holding is not about this mythical pleasantness. Instead it tries to shed light on another side of our beloved state: the inspired, bizarre, sometimes gruesome, brilliant, scandalous, and funny sites around Minnesota. After all, our state does have a lot to offer. Everyone talks about how beautiful California is—heck, we've got more shoreline than California, Florida, and Hawaii combined!

You want actors? We've got actors: Loni Anderson, Eddie Albert, Judy Garland, Jessica Lange, Robert Vaughn, even William Demarest (you know, Uncle Charlie in *My Three Sons*). We're like a Hollywood farm team! Tourists even take the Mary Tyler Moore tour of Minneapolis: a visit to "her house," an early morning power walk around Lake of the Isles, then a trip to Nicollet Mall, where they gleefully throw a knit beret into the air.

Ever heard of the Andrews Sisters? They're from Minneapolis. Patty, Laverne, and Maxine's Yiddish hit "Bei Mir Bist Du Schön" probably influenced all sorts of musicians from Dylan to Prince—by the way, they're from Minnesota, too. Of course the Seattle grunge craze was just a rip-off of local bands Soul Asylum, the Replacements, Babes in Toyland, and Hüsker Dü. Seattle just knows how to brag a little better than we do.

Crazy politicians? We've got them in spades! Just look at our recent governors, Rudy Perpich (dubbed "Governor Goofy" by *Newsweek*), Arne Carlson, and Jesse Ventura. Even the U.S. Communist Party hails from Minnesota.

And writers. You could spend every waking minute reading Minnesota authors such as F. Scott Fitzgerald, Laura Ingalls Wilder, Al Franken, Garrison Keillor, Sinclair Lewis, Meridel Le Sueur, Judith Guest, Bill Holm, O. E. Rolvaag, Winona LaDuke, and so on. One of our authors, Robert Bly, even inspired a generation of men to venture into the woods to howl, pound drums, and butt heads. Wow.

These are some of our celebrities, but what about the unsung visionaries? Ken Nyberg, who started welding enormous statues just for fun in tiny Vining; Ed Kruger, who refused to throw anything away; Ralph Samuelson, who dared walk on water; and Francis Johnson, who just kept wrapping twine, to name a few.

So here it is: the world's largest, the U.S. capital of so-and-so, strange museums, the nation's coldest, and one-of-a-kind tourist attractions. Diagnose us with an inferiority complex, call us braggarts, say what you will. Regardless, this is Minnesota.

Minnesota Marvels

Sure, Paul could crush you in his hand, but he's a good giant.

Akeley

World's Largest Paul Bunyan

Birthplace of Paul Bunyan

The story of Paul Bunyan's birth has yet to be written—perhaps the delivery of a giant doesn't make for a good yarn. Suffice it to say that Paul Bunyan's enormous umbilical cord was cut in the northern town of Akeley. Although Bemidji claims to be the birthplace of the world's greatest lumberjack, the proof is Paul's colossal cradle, which can be found in a small manger in the center of Akeley.

Paul's story was first put to paper by scribes for the Red River Lumber Company in Akeley in 1914, near the end of the heyday of Minnesota lumbering. According to the Minnesota Historical Society, W. B. Laughead and James Stevens threw truth to the wind and scrawled the tales, which had been exaggerated from one teller to the next. The lumber company published the myth in a promotional brochure touting "the largest sawmills in the world," with over seven hundred men piling twenty to thirty freight cars daily for the Red River Lumber Company.

As a tribute to the Minnesota lumberjack, the Krotzer family built the forty-two-foot high "World's Largest Paul Bunyan Statue" in 1984. Passersby can't help but take a photo of this mountain of fiberglass and climb into Paul's huge paw.

Once in Akeley, a quick tour through the "Complete History of Paul Bunyan" at the Red River Museum next door is a must.

At the end of June each year, the whole town lets its hair down to celebrate their native son during Paul Bunyan Days. Yodelin' Swede's Bar across the street is packed, and tourists line up to get their picture taken with Paul.

World's Largest Paul Bunyan. From Walker, take Highway 34 ten miles southwest to Akeley. The statue and museum are just past the intersection with Highway 64 on the north side of the road.

Albert Lea

Itasca Rock Garden
Castles and Trolls

John Christensen began cementing rocks together on a huge mound in his Itasca yard in 1925. Any vacation Christensen took would find him lugging back rocks and shells to add to his growing castle on the south end of the garden. Tourists eventually piled into what became the Itasca Rock Garden near Edgewater Park to walk the windy paths by mini–gnome houses, goldfish ponds, and blossoming flower beds.

According to legend, the little town of Itasca was meant to be the Freeborn county seat, but it lost to Albert Lea on a horse-race bet. Perhaps Christensen's castles and moats would still be in the limelight if Itasca's horse had won.

Christensen's Itasca Rock Garden faced competition when the Vogt brothers built the "Aksarben Garden" (backward for "Nebraska," their home state) up on Bay Lake, northwest of Garrison. After eighteen summers of building, the Vogt brothers lured celebrities such as Will Rogers, Clark Gable, and Norma Talmadge to pop twenty-five cents to tour Aksarben's towers, moat, waterfall, and wishing well. As an added attraction, the brothers would ring a little bell and all the bass on Tame Fish Lake would swim over for a snack, just like Pavlov's dog.

Both the Aksarben and Itasca Rock Gardens appeared on postcards and attracted hordes of tourists. Visitors to Albert Lea's Itasca went over and under little bridges amidst pungent flowers to find tiny trolls guarding their lawns and dwellings built into the hill. Christensen's masterpiece extended to his house's basement, where a fountain and rock garden jutted out from the foundation, doubling as a greenhouse.

Today, the Itasca Rock Garden is one of the famous and forgotten sites of Albert Lea. Although Christensen's lifetime work is now on private property, the owners keep up the bouquets of tiger lilies and sometimes allow visitors to take a peek.

Winding paths over and under bridges and around little castles seem intended only for hidden trolls, but Albert Lea's rock garden has hosted tourists from across the state.

Itasca Rock Garden. From Albert Lea, take Highway 13 toward Blue Earth, then turn right on County Road 101. Don't enter Edgewater Park, but turn left at the fork, then left again at the "T" in the road (private residence).

While in the Area

Waterskiers splash by downtown Albert Lea in the heat of summer on nearby Fountain Lake. To promote the city's Danish heritage, a loose replica of Copenhagen's Little Mermaid, made famous by Hans Christian Andersen, is perched on a small rock offshore (and provides slalom for skiers).

Not only does Marion Ross—Mrs. Cunningham from *Happy Days*—hail from here, but Eddie Cochran also called Albert Lea home. Although Eddie left town at the age of fourteen and never looked back, those sun-soaked days on the lake inspired him to strum "Summertime Blues" and "C'mon Everybody." Every June, a huge Eddie Cochran Festival is thrown with drive-in movies, car shows, museum tours, and occasional performances by The Kelly Four, Eddie's old band. Cochran never performed in Albert Lea, but according to locals, he was on his way home from England when he died in a car wreck in 1960. His body ended up in California.

Local tradition calls for high schoolers to wade in the water to cover up the town temptress flaunting her bosom to the scandalized teens. Just an hour after I took this photo, revelers undressed the poor little Danish mermaid.

Alexandria

Kensington Runestone
Birthplace of America

Olaf Ohman's ten-year-old son was digging by the edge of a swamp near their Kensington home in 1898 when he struck an enormous tablet with bizarre scribbles all over it. His father recognized the unusual symbols as Nordic runes. Nine years after the stone was discovered, the cryptic text was finally unraveled, revealing that the Vikings had beaten Columbus to the New World:

> Eight Goths and 22 Norwegians on an exploration journey from Vinland to the west. We had camp by 2 skerries one day's journey north from this stone. We were to fish one day after we came home found 10 men red of blood and dead AVM [Ave Maria].

> [On the side of the stone] We have 10 men by the sea to look after our ships 14 days' travel from this island Year 1362.

The mysterious stone traveled around the country and even appeared for a brief stint in the Smithsonian Institution. The curators wrote, "The Smithsonian Institution has appointed no commission, but states, 'Perhaps the most widely known object attributed to the Vikings is the Kensington Runestone.'"

Controversy ensued as scholars lined up to debunk the stone, finding it suspect that Scandinavian immigrants discovered a stone claiming their relatives were here centuries earlier.

Most everyone was convinced it was a fake when it was revealed that Olaf Ohman had long been interested in runes and that his neighbor, minister Sven Fogelblad, had studied Nordic writing. Ohman had read many books on runes and was even a trained stonemason. That was enough to convince critics that the pair probably forged the writing as an elaborate hoax for a good laugh.

Professor Erik Wahlgren, an expert in the Norwegian language,

Looming over downtown Alexandria, Big Ole was built to accompany the Kensington Runestone to the 1965 New York World's Fair.

claimed, "The Swedish on the stone was a version of that language that had never been spoken anywhere outside the American Midwest." A few mistakes on the stone made critics think they had used modern Swedish grammar, some particular to Ohman's own Halsingland dialect.

The stone ended up back in Minnesota and the residents of Alexandria recognized a tourist attraction when they saw it. Big Ole, the Viking statue, was raised to lure tourists and school field trips into the new Runestone Museum. Inside, displays of ancient Scandinavian mooring stones and fire steels found nearby support the runestone's claims and teach children that the Vikings were the first Europeans in Minnesota.

Hjalmar Holand, the stone's strongest advocate, proposed a theory on the origin of the runestone. In 1355, the evangelical Catholic King Magnus Erickson of Sweden and Norway hadn't heard word from his colonies in Greenland and Vinland (North America), so he sent an expedition led by Paul Knutson to make sure that the word of Christianity was still alive. Knutson found the colony in Greenland deserted, so he continued on to Vinland. One winter, the explorers were icebound in Hudson Bay and the following summer a small party went down the Nelson River into Lake Winnipeg and onto the Red River. A group returned from a fishing trip one day and found ten of their mates killed by Indians. The runestone was left as a message to their other companions. The crew members waiting on Hudson Bay eventually returned to Norway in 1363 or 1364, while their companions in Minnesota abandoned hope of making it back. Instead, they settled in North Dakota with the Mandan Indian tribe, which explains the blue eyes and fair skin of the Mandans, their European-style towns, and the runic images found on old Mandan animal bones.

The Minneapolis *Star Tribune* published its opinion in 1992: "The combination of historical, factual, physical, and philological evidence fits together in a logical manner to prove that the Runestone is genuine. On the other hand, in order to believe it is a fake, it is necessary to believe a whole series of things that range from the extremely improbable to the flat-out impossible."

The curator of the beautiful Runestone Museum in downtown Alexandria is almost offended when tourists ask about the stone's validity. "Anybody from Alexandria believes it's real," she states matter-of-factly. "The Smithsonian is doing a Viking exhibit, and they want it on loan. They're this close to proving that it's real."

A tour guide for the museum says, "Some say that Christopher Columbus was an outcast and had traveled to Norway, where the New World was common knowledge," adding, "I'm Irish, but I'm still a believer. I don't think you have to be Scandinavian to believe."

Runestone Museum and Old Fort Alexandria, 206 Broadway, (320) 763-3160. From I-94, take Highway 29 north into Alexandria. Look for the big Viking statue on Main Street (Broadway).

Austin

The Spam Museum

The "Miracle Meat" Mecca

Venture inside an enormous can of Spam just north of downtown, and you've discovered the First Century Historical Hormel Foods Museum, or simply "The Spam Museum." Marvel at the very first canned ham, the vats of Hormel shortening, and the resourceful use of pork products in everything from Spam-n-Tongue to Deviled Spam Curds.

Laugh you may, but according to Sandra Gurvis in *America's Strangest Museums,* "If all the cans ever eaten were placed end-to-end, they would circle the globe at least ten times." Besides, Hormel is the twenty-fourth largest food company in the United States, raking in an estimated three billion dollars a year. Although the historical photos of the "Hog Kill Gang," the "Meat Cooler Gang," the "Lard Room," and the "Ham Boning Room" may seem crude, the folks in them put Austin on the map.

Though no mention is made in the museum of the long labor strikes during the 1980s, much attention is given to comptroller Cy Thomson, who was put through business college by founder George Hormel and then embezzled nearly $1,200,000 by 1916. See the checking deposit slips that nearly ruined the company!

Hormel rebounded and how. The twenty-member "Hormel Chili Beaners" song-and-dance group (organized by the founder's son, Jay Hormel) hit the road to promote their new chili. In 1937, he created another sensation with a little extra pork shoulder, a smidgen of chopped ham, a dash of secret spices and abracadabra! "Spam"—short for "spiced ham"—was born!

Spam eventually saved the world by winning World War II. Slammin' Spammy, the fighting pig, went to war, feeding the troops by making the ultimate sacrifice. Sure, doughboys may have turned Spam's nickname, the "miracle meat," into the "mystery meat that failed the physical," but it was probably a welcome break from K rations.

11

Our allies also appreciated the canned Minnesota pigs. In 1942, Edward R. Murrow reported, "This is London. Although the Christmas table won't be lavish, there will be Spam for everyone."

Even Dwight Eisenhower gave Hormel a backhanded compliment in a postwar letter: "During World War II, of course, I ate my share of SPAM along with millions of other soldiers. I'll even confess to a few unkind remarks about it—uttered during the strain of battle, you understand. But as former Commander in Chief, I believe I can still officially forgive you your only sin: sending us so much."

At the time, little was said about Hormel's aid to the Russians. Nevertheless, Nikita Khrushchev sang Spam's praises: "There are many jokes going around in the army, some of them off-color, about American Spam; it tasted good nonetheless. Without Spam, we wouldn't have been able to feed our army."

Postwar, Hormel hoped to keep GIs hooked. The official company drum-and-bugle corps was dropped in favor of the luscious "Hormel Girls." Once wartime austerity measures were halted, their thirty-five-car caravan of sixty women traveled thirty thousand miles a year between 1948 and 1953, singing the songs of Spam.

The marketing blitz raged on with radio ads by George Burns and Gracie Allen stumping for Spam. Hormel even says that the first radio jingle—sung by Clelland Card on WCCO radio—was for Spam. General Mills makes the same claim for Wheaties.

Hormel knew that merchandising was half the game. Prizes and premiums were offered, including chili can radios, Spam cigarette lighters, Spam blankets, Spam radios, Spam flashlights, Spam watches, Spam lunchboxes, and Spam thermoses. More products hit the supermarket shelves, such as Spam and Cheese, Cured Pork Tongue, Smoke-Flavored Spam, and even Spam Pizza. The Spam Racing Team showed the world that pork meant power.

Spam's popularity has waned in recent years, but that didn't stop Boris Yeltsin from showing his love for pork when he toured Austin in 1992. The company president is pictured proudly handing a complimentary can of Spam to the glassy-eyed Russian president (maybe it was just jet lag).

The soundtrack of the museum is a continuous loop of Hormel TV ads plugging the miracle meat, which is featured on restaurant menus all over town. Jerry's Other Place at 1207 North Main Street serves Spam-n-Eggs. Tolly's Time Out at 100 Fourteenth Street SW whips up Spamburgers and the specialty of the house, Spam Supreme, featuring grilled Spam, onions, and tomatoes, all smothered in melted American cheese.

Spam Museum, corner of North Main Street and Spam Boulevard, 1937 Spam Boulevard, (800) LUV-SPAM. Take the Sixth Street exit off of I-90. Turn south and go toward the factory. At the "T" turn right, then stay right at the fork. Just past the bridge is the museum.

Beaver Bay

Split Rock Lighthouse State Park
On the Lake They Call Gitchee Gumee

The stretch of coast northeast of Two Harbors has been considered by some seafarers to be the most dangerous area in the world. Because of huge underwater iron ore deposits, compasses are unreliable on Lake Superior, so when fog sets in, ships can be lost at sea.

On November 28, 1905, a storm blew through Gitchee Gumee, ravaging twenty-nine ships. U.S. Steel was hit hard; they owned most of the damaged vessels and hadn't insured them. To protect the remainder of its fleet, the huge company lobbied Congress to build a lighthouse on top of the treacherous Split Rock Cliff. In 1907, the U.S. government appropriated $75,000 to build a state-of-the-art lighthouse. Since the area was accessible only by boat, an old-fashioned crane hauled 310 tons of construction material up the sheer 130-foot cliff. Eventually, tram tracks were laid ascending at a more than 45-degree angle to lug supplies up the hill.

By 1910, construction was complete. A huge bivalve lens magnified an oil vapor lamp, casting the light more than twenty miles out on the lake. In case of poor visibility, huge air compressors were fired up to feed the foghorns, which could be heard many miles away.

Due to modern navigational equipment, Split Rock was deemed obsolete by the Coast Guard in 1969. The lighthouse lamp is still lit every November 10 to mark the anniversary of the 1975 sinking of the *Edmund Fitzgerald.*

The Minnesota Historical Society now manages Split Rock, offering tours of the light keeper's house, the fog signal building, and, of course, the lighthouse itself. A gift shop and interpretive center shed light on the lake and its navigational dangers. Occasionally, guides

Modern navigational equipment has rendered the Split Rock Lighthouse obsolete, but during its heyday it saved numerous ships from banging into cliffs in what was considered one of the most dangerous stretches of water in the world.

To honor Silver Bay as the Taconite Capital of the World, Rocky Taconite was built by Village & Reserve Mining Company in 1964, and now greets visitors at the entrance to this Lake Superior town north of the Split Rock Lighthouse.

dress up in period costumes to get the feel of the old days, when ships bashed into the rocks below.

Split Rock Lighthouse, (218) 226-6377. Take Highway 61 north of Two Harbors about twenty miles. Look for signs to Split Rock Lighthouse on the right. Summer only.

Belle Plaine

Home of the Two-Story Outhouse
Historic Privy Skyscraper

A two-story biffy has become the symbol of Belle Plaine. The historic Hooper-Bowler-Hill house contains a beautifully kept, working version of the 1871 outhouse, and tour guides explain that the impressive five-holer was essential for the huge family that lived there.

This architectural wonder was tacked on to the rest of the house, but at a distance to prevent unwanted fumes from entering inside. The covered "skyway" (the world's first?) on the second story allowed toilet-goers to avoid stepping outside. But what about the poor souls downstairs? The outhouse is ingeniously designed with the top floor set back to avoid the delivery of unwelcome surprises to those below.

Anyone in town can give directions to the biffy. Although Belle Plaine calls itself "The Home of the Two-Story Outhouse" and has T-shirts to prove it, some locals tend to downplay it. When asked about the landmark, a carp fisherman next to the Minnesota River avoided bragging, saying only, "Yeah, I suppose it is famous, ya know."

Two-Story Outhouse, Hooper-Bowler-Hill House, 410 North Cedar Street (at East Court Street), (952) 873-4433 or (952) 873-6109. From Highway 169 take the Belle Plaine exit north into town and look for the old white house next to the town park.

While in the Area

For something completely different, stop by Schumacher's Hotel for a posh Old World experience in a classy, renovated brick building designed by Cass Gilbert. While dining in style on Czech cuisine, don't miss the hand-carved bar stools, which look like hikers' legs.

Schumacher's Hotel, 212 West Main Street, New Prague, (952) 758-2133 or (800) 283-2049.

Rather than freezing their toes running outside in the snow, a skyway let the children of the Hooper-Bowler-Hill house scurry to the second floor of the biffy. The ingenious architects offset the top floor to avoid treasures from heaven raining down on those beneath.

Bemidji

Fireplace of the States

Stones from Sea to Shining Sea

A local resort owner with a penchant for tall tales started building a showpiece fireplace in the 1930s, collecting rocks to add to his chimney whenever he'd go on vacation. Stones from Yellowstone Park and Old Fort Gray in Winnipeg were cemented in alongside dinosaur bones and fossilized sloth tracks. He spun yarns about each stone's origin and curious travelers began stopping by to hear his fantastic tales.

Letters were sent across the country asking for new rocks to complete the collection. As the fireplace gained notoriety, governors and politicians plopped postage stamps on bricks from landmarks such as the Statue of Liberty, FDR's house in Hyde Park, New York, and the U.S. Capitol, all bound for Bemidji. States around the union wanted to be represented at the country's most famous fireplace. What began as a whim became a nationwide effort, with rocks arriving from all forty-eight states (Hawaii and Alaska weren't states at the time).

The "Fireplace of the States" was completed in 1937, and Paul Bunyan's personal effects now rest on the mantelpiece: his immense razor and toothpaste, his oversized CB radio, and his huge boxers, moccasins, and Zippo lighter.

Fireplace of the States, Bemidji Avenue and Third Street (218) 751-3540 or 1-800-292-2223. Take Highway 197 (Paul Bunyan Drive) right into town by Lake Bemidji and look for the Paul Bunyan statue. The Fireplace of the States is inside the tourist center.

The Fireplace of the States in Bemidji claims a stone from every state in the Union and most Canadian provinces.

Bemidji

The Original Paul Bunyan

Symbol of the American Worker

Although Akeley may have been Paul Bunyan's birthplace, Bemidji put the giant on the map. In 1937, self-important Bemidji mayor Earl Bucklen posed for a woodcutter's statue made three times his size for the Bemidji Winter Carnival. This towering lumberjack has become the quintessential Paul Bunyan, overlooking Lake Bemidji at eighteen feet tall and weighing two and a half tons.

Paul never moved, but the county highway department built a "portable" Babe the Blue Ox of wire, wood, and canvas, perching him on top of an old Model T for the carnival parade. An enormous exhaust pipe was hooked up to his nose, making huge clouds of smoke come out. The parade nearly came to a halt, though, when Babe's tin horns kept pulling down strings of Christmas decorations hanging over the streets. The ox-hauling Tin Lizzie then toured the nation, with flattering photos appearing in the *New York Times* and *Life* magazine. Attendance at the Bemidji parade skyrocketed from 15,000 in 1937 to 100,000 the following year according to the *Bemidji Daily Pioneer.*

Life on the road took its toll, however, and the worn-down Babe returned home to his master's side by Lake Bemidji. A local boat company gave the ox a facelift and a tummy tuck, adding huge wooden ribs and setting the front legs far enough apart for a truck to be driven underneath. Car headlights were mounted in his eyes, and a smoking pipe was set in his nostrils to show the true power of the mighty beast.

Babe's owner also changed with the times. In John Dos Passos's 1932 book *Nineteen Nineteen,* Paul Bunyan was portrayed as a strong union man. He became a symbol of "the American worker," says historian Karal Ann Marling, "grown larger-than-life in the strength of collective action."

Carl Sandburg also stumped for Paul in his 1936 book, *The People, Yes,* where he said that "the people" had created this gentle giant:

"The anonymous folk concocted Paul Bunyan out of the genial humor of their collective imagination and their mutual resilience of spirit."

From his beginnings in the colorful advertising brochures for the Red River Lumber Company, Paul has been used to promote many causes, large and small. He has been a fearless labor leader and a shill for the "Bunyan Burger" at the Burger House in Bemidji; he has been a symbol for the hardy Minnesota work ethic and a logo at the Paul Bunyan Putt-Putt Park. In 1958, Walt Disney even produced a short animated movie, *Paul Bunyan,* which showed children how Minnesota's lakes were created by this cartoon Goliath.

While most stories glorify the overgrown logger, some vilify him for his lack of concern for the environment. An Ojibwe legend describes how the Native American Nanabojo challenged Paul Bunyan to a duel

At eighteen feet tall, Paul Bunyan looms over Lake Bemidji alongside Babe, who was originally perched on top of an old Model T (to be hauled around to town festivals).

since the lumberjack was too greedy and had stripped too many forests of trees. As the story goes, Nanabojo and Paul fought for weeks, and the Indian eventually beat Paul to death with a huge fish.

A huge fiberglass statue of Shaynowishkung, "Chief Bemidji," stands across the street, facing the Paul Bunyan statue in an eternal stare down. Chief Bemidji helped the first settlers in the region make it through the tough winters, so this enormous statue was raised in his honor (and to lure some visitors into the nearby tourist shop).

Paul and Babe still keep watch over Bemidji and remain the heaviest and most photographed fiberglass in town, weighing in at a hefty five tons. According to the Bemidji tourism office, 6,300 people a day stop by to say "hi" to the lumberjack and his blue friend (but then they also claim Paul could eat thirty-six pancakes a day).

Paul Bunyan and Babe the Blue Ox, Bemidji Avenue and Third Street (218) 751-3540 or 1-800-292-2223. From Highway 2, take Highway 197 (Paul Bunyan Drive) right into the center of town. Look for the statues on the east side of the road next to Lake Bemidji.

Bena

Big Fish Supper Club
Drive-In Muskie

When Butch Dahl was just a kid looking for some odd jobs in the summer of 1958, he got roped into the strangest one he could imagine: building a big fish.

The Leech Lake Indian Reservation is famous for angling; in fact, the state's largest muskie was caught in nearby Lake Winnibigoshish. This passion for fish, along with the drive-in rage of the 1950s, inspired a bold Bena entrepreneur to construct "The Big Muskie Drive-In."

Dahl remembers, "We took one-by-fours, soaked 'em in water and bent 'em for the ribs." The fish's frame extends sixty-five feet and reaches fourteen feet into the air. "We nailed on sheets of tar paper over the ribs, and slapped on a coat of paint," Dahl says. After the long teeth were carved, he recalls, "We needed some eyes. We looked around and found a couple of Coca-Cola signs." The round red Coke signs still stare out at the highway.

The Big Muskie was open for just a couple of years as a drive-in with a little take-out window on the side. For a while, tourists could walk into its mouth to buy souvenirs, but tar paper isn't made to last through northern Minnesota winters.

The Big Fish is now merely a storage shack, but according to the owner, "We have to paint it almost every year, you know." The former drive-in looks like it's in great shape, and it still lures tourists off the road to snap a photo.

The fish's fame extends beyond Minnesota, having appeared in one of the National Lampoon *Vacation* movies with Chevy Chase, in Charles Kuralt's television series, and in many magazines, such as *Ranger Rick* and *Muppet Magazine*.

In the spirit of old photo collage postcards, the owner remembers, "One day these two spear fishermen stop in and want to know if they can use a ladder to climb up on top of the fish for a photo!"

"Please Don't Steal the Teeth!" reads the sign on the door to the Big Fish in Bena.

In spite of this fame, she is fed up with the fish. After twenty-nine years of upkeep, she wants to sell it and retire. "What can I say good about it?" she asks. "It's a pain, not a moneymaker." Even so, her attached Big Fish Supper Club is usually packed with winter snowmobilers or summer fishermen.

Big Fish Supper Club, (218) 665-2333. Go west of Bena one mile on Highway 2.

Convenience stores are few and far between on Highway 2 on the Leech Lake Indian Reservation, but Bena has a red, white, and blue gas station looking more like a pagoda than a typical Minnesota log cabin.

Bloomington

The Mall of America
Shopping Space Station

Southdale, built in Edina in 1956, was the world's first enclosed two-story shopping mall, but Bloomington's Mall of America is the biggest. Spanning 4.2 million square feet with more than four hundred stores, the "Mega-Mall" is "like the difference between a space station and a bus station," wrote the *New York Times* when the mall opened in 1992.

In spite of cynics' predictions, "the Mall" is here to stay. With its aquarium, roller coaster, shops, restaurants, marriage chapel, and school, why should anyone ever leave? During the winter, many shut-ins cure their cabin fever by meandering around the warm, spacious hallways all day. Rather than spring for a charter flight to Cancun, you can munch on tropical fare at the Rainforest Café amidst simulated exotic plants and piped-in thunderstorms.

Tourists jet in from around the world to experience Minnesota by splashing down the forty-foot waterfall at Paul Bunyan's Log Chute or witnessing a "movie adventure" by spelunking through the Mystery Mine Ride, reminiscent of the Iron Range. But their main objective is to shop.

To the chagrin of merchants in Minneapolis and St. Paul, the Mall of America has become the most famous landmark in the state. The Mega-Mall was pictured as a shopping mecca on *The Simpsons,* and the *Onion* newspaper ran a story with the headline, "Federal Seat of Power Moves to Mall of America" in 1997. According to the article, the government wanted to get back in touch with America's consumers, prompting Newt Gingrich to declare, "Finally, Congress, the Supreme Court and Foot Locker are all under one roof!"

Mall of America, 60 East Broadway, (952) 883-8800. The Mall is located at the crossroads of Interstate 494 and Highway 77 (Cedar

A well-fed, blow-up statue of Charles Schulz's famous pooch jiggles with glee as the centerpiece of this indoor city's mini-Disneyland, Knott's Camp Snoopy.

Avenue). From Interstate 35W, go east on Interstate 494, then south at Twenty-Fourth Avenue. From I-494 westbound, take the Twenty-Fourth Avenue exit south. From Highway 77, exit on either Eighty-First Street/Lindau Lane or Killebrew Drive.

Bloomington

Thunderbird Motel

Totem Pole Dining Room and Pow-wow Lounge

The image of the thunderbird was emblazoned into raw stone five thousand years ago on Jeffer's Petroglyphs in southwestern Minnesota. Vigorously flapping its wings, the bird shoots thunder and lightning from its eyes. These striking images stretch back to the Late Archaic–Early Woodland period. The Thunderbird Hotel on the 494 strip in Bloomington claims to have preserved Indian images like this with its fiberglass statues from the mid-1970s period.

Small sculptures of Shoshone, Iroquois, Cree, Blackfeet, Dakota, and Choctaw Indians, as well as birch-bark canoes and a little papoose, create a "Distinctive Native American motif," as the hotel calls it. Stuffed coyote, lynx, brown bear, buffalo, moose, elk, wolf, and rattlesnakes add to the theme.

Upstairs, past a fountain with a wooden statue of an Indian chief, is the "Hall of Tribes," where animal heads stare down at businessmen and women heading for meetings in the "Winnebago room," the "Cherokee room," the "Pawnee room," and the "Menominee room."

The owners of the hotel and its many Indian-themed items, however, are not Native American. A group of Minnesota social studies teachers decided that, partially because of this, the collection was in bad taste. The teachers agreed to spend more money to hold their annual conference at a different hotel. "The Thunderbird Hotel uses the image of Native Americans to draw in customers and make money," one educator said. "It's incredibly disrespectful of their traditions."

The hotel has been unfazed by the flack and keeps running its Bow and Arrow Coffee Shop, the Totem Pole Dining Room, the Peace Pipe Gift Shop, and the incredibly camp Pow-wow Lounge.

Three huge fiberglass statues rise over the hotel. The largest bare-chested Indian salutes the traffic passing on the freeway below. The second is said to represent the Chippewa (Ojibwe) tribe, who, the description says, "often fought the Souix (sic) and Fox tribes. . . .

As "part of far northern Indian tradition," the totem pole of the Thunderbird Hotel is used to draw tourists into its suites, designed with a Native American motif.

Members tried to gain long life by using herbs and magic." And the third fiberglass statue, covered with brass paint, stands in front of the hotel entrance. It's Chief Thunderbird, a symbol of the past.

Thunderbird Hotel, 2201 East Seventy-Eighth Street, (952) 854-3411. From I-494, take the Twenty-Fourth Avenue exit south. Look for the totem pole on the southwest corner of the intersection.

Blue Earth

The Jolly Green Giant

Shoe Size: 78, Smile: 48 Inches Long

Tourist brochures wax poetic: "Rising out of the sea of corn and peas against the disappearing horizons swirling around Blue Earth is the world's tallest statue of the Jolly Green Giant. . . . His legendary 'Ho Ho Ho' has boomed over this rolling farmland of the Blue Earth Area since July 6, 1979." Minnesota's southern prairie is ruled by this green colossus—half vegetable, half human—towering fifty-five and a half feet over the countryside. As a personification of O. E. Rolvaag's *Giants in the Earth,* the human-like Jolly Green Giant skyscraper testifies to the power of the plant to make a small town prosperous.

After a quick look around, tourists soon notice that the Jolly Green Giant's little buddy, Sprout, is conspicuously missing. Sprout stood only three feet tall and was born in 1973 as Jolly's TV sidekick.

Alison at the adjacent Dairy Queen knows the scoop about Sprout's demise. "See, there's this big rivalry between our town and Fairmont. So, the day after Fairmont soundly beat Blue Earth in a football game, I came to work at the DQ. I was like 'Oh, oh' since I noticed Sprout was missing. I just knew that those guys from Fairmount stole Sprout in a postgame celebration." Even the Jolly Green Giant's eight thousand pounds couldn't intimidate those ruffians.

The young dairy queen explains that "Blue Earth got Fairmont back in a basketball match," but Fairmont then took their revenge out on Sprout. "The day after the game," she says, "I called up my fiancé and told him, 'You'll never guess who I saw hanging from the overpass!' I was driving down the interstate and saw Sprout's head hanging from the overpass. Those guys from Fairmont had cut his head off!"

Obviously unconcerned about these real-life bandits on the low plains, the clerks at the Jolly Green Giant gift store at the foot of the titan were munching enormous burgers, absorbed in a shoot-'em-up TV program. When asked about poor Sprout, they said only "Oh,

Welcome To The Valley
Blue Earth Mn.

Decked out in a biker vest, the Jolly Green Giant gets ready
for a biker weekend—he just needs a two-story Harley Hog
for a trek to Sturgis.

some kids stole him. They were supposed to have finished a second one months ago, but still nothing."

In spite of this apathy, the Jolly Green Giant puts on his forty-eight-inch smile, hoping for the best. Perhaps none of this would have happened if he had kept the image he originally had when he first appeared on a bag of beans in 1925—that of a menacing white giant covered by an enormous bearskin. The Minnesota Valley Canning Company deemed that character, based on a Grimm's fairy tale, too menacing, so they softened him to create a more positive corporate image.

The "Green Giant" name evolved from a type of long, wrinkled pea pod developed in England, which the U.S. patent office allowed the Blue Earth Canning Company to copyright after the Jolly Green Giant logo appeared. In 1929, the Blue Earth Canning Company became part of Minnesota Valley Canning, based in Le Sueur, the mythical "Valley of the Jolly Green Giant." Even though Green Giant was later bought by Pillsbury, then Grand Met, and now Seneca Foods, the Jolly Green Giant has remained the town symbol of Blue Earth.

The statue was the brainchild of radio station owner Paul Hedberg. He got on his bully pulpit on the radio and preached for a green beast to tower over Blue Earth. While skeptics ranted, eleven local businesses stepped forward, pitching in at least five thousand dollars each.

The deadline for completing the statue was set for September 24, 1978, to coincide with the completion of the coast-to-coast I-90 freeway, converging in Blue Earth. Creative Displays of Sparta, Wisconsin, came to the rescue and met the deadline. In a mere eight weeks, the $1,000-a-foot giant was ready and trucked down the interstate on September 23. The governor, Miss Minnesota, and Miss America were on hand to watch the erection of the giant and the joining of the east and west coasts in Blue Earth.

In an attempt to recreate the symbolism of the golden spike that was used to complete the cross-country railway in 1869, Blue Earth used "imported gold paint from Germany" to paint a strip of concrete at the rest stop just west of town. The historical reference was overshadowed by the enormous Jolly Green Giant looking down on the whole scene. Nature versus technology.

While the giant's friend Sprout may have been kidnapped by the malcontents of Fairmont, the Blue Earth Chamber of Commerce says the dull golden cement on the interstate is safe: "I don't think they could steal that one!"

Jolly Green Giant. Go south of I-90 on Highway 169 a few blocks. Look up for the giant on the right side of the road.

Bongards

Humongous Holstein

Milk the Fiberglass Cow

A huge Holstein cow sculpture stands in the tiny "co-op town" (as opposed to corporate town) of Bongards, just north of the two-story outhouse in Belle Plaine. Bongards Creamery was set up as a co-operative for all the dairy farmers in the region, and they all chipped in for this huge Holstein to draw customers into the little dairy store across the street.

The enormous cow story dates back to W. B. Laughead's original tales of Paul Bunyan and Lucy the Cow, who munched on pine trees instead of measly hay. Lumberjacks would line up to milk the mutant bovine, reaching over their heads to the huge udders. Rather than rich cream, however, Lucy pumped out liniment that the woodsmen spread on their aching muscles to soothe the pain. Could Bongards's cow be the long-lost love of Babe the Blue Ox, whose emasculation forced Lucy to seek greener pastures?

F.A.S.T. (Fiberglass Animals, Shapes, and Trademarks) of Sparta, Wisconsin, made the mold for the cow and plopped it on a flatbed, destination Bongards. While just a heifer compared to the "World's Largest Holstein" towering above the plains of New Salem, North Dakota, and not nearly as exotic as Neillsville, Wisconsin's "Chatty Belle," the black and white bovine serves its purpose, luring farmers and tourists to the co-op. At this point, there are no plans to attach rubber udders so kids can milk the fake cow. Probably enough real ones in the area to be milked.

Bongards Creamery says it's been making "Premium Cheese since 1942," all with the "Real Dairy" logo, so ignore the "Pasteurized Cheese Food with Processed Vegetables" in the fridge of the dairy store and head for the delicious extra-sharp cheddar. Even the lactose intol-

Bovine growth hormones gone awry! In the tiny town of Bongards, a huge cow could feed thousands.

erant have something to buy since Bongards sells fluffy "Roly-Poly" cows just like the huge Holstein outside.

Bongards Creamery (and Cow), 13200 County Road 51, (952) 466-5521. Between Cologne and Norwood on Highway 212, look for signs to Bongards and go south two hundred yards on Highway 51.

Brainerd

Paul Bunyan Amusement Center
World's Largest Talking Paul Bunyan

"That Paul Bunyan is one smart lumberjack!" yells a happy little girl when Brainerd's seemingly psychic giant guesses her name and hometown. Another boy is bawling as the twenty-six-foot-high wood-cutting beast bellows out, "Hello, Tommy from Burnsville!" Ignore the man behind the log cabin and the cashier with the microphone feeding him information. The site is the Paul Bunyan Amusement Center at the southern end of the Paul Bunyan Trail.

Brainerd was settled in 1870 by railroad agent "Pussy" White. It soon boomed as a hub for transporting lumber by rail, not to mention as a rendezvous for workers wanting to whoop it up. In the summer of 1935, Brainerd hosted the first Paul Bunyan Water Carnival with guests of honor Paul and Pauline marching down Main Street.

Following the huge success of the parade, Brainerd resident Art Lyonais put up the cash to build the first statue to commemorate the famous lumberjack. Moira Harris, author of *Monumental Minnesota*, says, "The artist is unknown (he was said to have been a transient who lived under the Brainerd bridge)." The statue still stands in front of the tourist information office at the corner of Highways 371 and 210.

In 1949, as the cold war was beginning to heat up, Chicago and Northwestern Railroad built a twenty-six-foot-high talking Paul Bunyan in honor of its brisk lumber business, while Mother Russia was busy constructing its cement versions of Lenin and Stalin. Historian Karal Ann Marling suggests that Brainerd's Paul Bunyan is an obvious parody of the Lincoln Memorial.

Whatever its politics, the talking Paul Bunyan was a hit, and Sherman Levis and Ray Kuemicheal purchased Paul from the railroad and opened Paul Bunyan Land in 1950. Bemidji cried foul, since it already claimed the lumberjack as its own. Brainerd simply ignored its

BRAINERD, MN.

The lumberjack's head twists, his hands move, and his mouth opens to amaze the kids by guessing their names and hometowns. Ignore the man behind the log cabin!

neighbor's gripe and began rewriting history with new Paul Bunyan anecdotes.

Brainerd stole Bemidji's steam and started naming everything after its most famous son: the Paul Bunyan Expressway, the Paul Bunyan Bowl, the Paul Bunyan (Bike) Trail, Pauline's Restaurant, the Paul Bunyan Nature Center, and so forth. A new series of chainsaw sculptures was even commissioned to commemorate Paul Bunyan's early days. Laurel Street in downtown Brainerd has statues of Baby Paul, Paul at six years old, and the lumberjack as a young man.

Citizens of Brainerd scored a coup in the 1990s when Joel and Ethan Coen of St. Louis Park chose their town for the movie *Fargo* ("Brainerd" didn't sound right as the title of a film apparently). While locals are still upset that the Minnesota accent was overdone, perhaps more troubling is that the Paul Bunyan chainsaw statue in the movie didn't end up in town. Instead, the Coen brothers donated the relatively small Paul to the tiny town of Hensel, North Dakota, for their help with the movie. Tourists in Brainerd ask about the statue, only to discover that it's not even in Minnesota.

But who needs another little statue when Brainerd already has one that weighs five thousand pounds, has sixteen-inch eyes, and wears size eighty boots? After all, Brainerd was "Paul Bunyan's Playground," and now has the nation's most photographed statue (or so they claim).

Today, youngsters can walk into Paul Bunyan Land, passing the impressive Blue Ox nestled among the pickups in the parking lot: "This is no bull, this is Babe the Blue Ox." To buy tickets for the rides, stroll by the huge chain fence—which happens to be Paul's weighty necklace. That crater you just stepped into was Paul Bunyan's footprint—imagine the mess if Paul got into a foul mood.

Once inside, even adults are dwarfed by Paul's immense ax, phone, toothpaste, Zippo lighter, and giant magic mushrooms. Henry the Giant Squirrel, the critter who munched on prune pits at Paul's legendary logging camp on the Big Onion River, is also there. Sport the Reversible Dog keeps Henry from getting too frisky. Since the canine was cut in half crosswise and sewn back together upside down, when he gets too tired, he just flips upside down and keeps on trucking.

At the back of this surreal scene is the man of the hour, Paul Bunyan, in a huge split-log crèche. The giant who knows all can wow the crowd of tots as he nods, blinks, and tells tall tales of the old logging days.

Paul Bunyan Amusement Center, junction of Highways 210 and 371 on the northeast corner, (218) 829-6342. From downtown Brainerd, go west on Highway 371 over the Mississippi and past a series of strip malls. The amusement park is on the right side, where Highway 371 turns north and Highway 210 continues. Summer only.

Burnsville

Fantasuite Hotel

"Blast Off in Our Space Capsule Waterbed!"

When you think of Burnsville, "romantic" doesn't usually pop to mind, but the Quality Inn "Fantasuite Hotel" wants to change that. Each room has an exotic theme designed to ignite a little love between any couple (costumes not provided).

In the Moby Dick room, guests are invited to "sleep in a queen-size whaling dinghy waterbed before venturing into the mouth of the great white whale."

Imagine saving on costly airfare to faraway Italy by taking a short drive to the suburbs. In Caesar's Court, brochures boast, "Roman murals and decor accent a two-person marble whirlpool." In the Venetian Holiday room, you can "Float your cares away in a queen-size waterbed Gondola." No need to worry about pickpockets lightening your load, or pesky mafiosi ruining your vacation!

The harem theme plays strong in the Desert Nights and Arabian Nights rooms, where a man can "Relax like a sheik in a tented room." If that's not enough, stay in the Pharaoh's Chamber and "Languish inside a pyramid. . . . King Tut watches over all who stay here . . . overlooking murals of the Nile & the Sphinx."

Another favorite is the Eastern Winds room, where "geisha fans and mirrors are just a prelude to the huge tile volcano like lava flow whirlpool. The queen size waterbed will have you never wanting to say Sianara [sic]."

Perhaps the most exotic of all, though, is the Jungle Safari: "Look out for the wild animals! A Thatch hut . . . Tiki logs and huge tiled whirlpool in the jungle cave."

Let's hope Hal the computer obeys in the Space Odyssey: "Blast off in our space capsule 7' round bed, complete with TV/VCR & original Nintendo game. A moonrock tiled whirlpool and murals of outerspace complete the out-of-this-world fantasy!"

While kids love the elaborate forts in every room, they're not intended for child's play. In the Castle Suite, for example, you are warned to "Beware of the FUN you can have in this dungeon of pleasure. A king size bed guarded by a shining knight in armor . . . surrounded by your favorite night romping creatures!" Complete with a "slipper" whirlpool, the suite features a "golden carriage" as "your queen bed with TV/VCR drawn by a white stallion."

For the more nostalgic, there's Lover's Leap, where you can "Relive the days in the park with that special person," using "a bed inside our '73 Olds convertible." Or for a journey further into the past, camp out in the Wild West, with "a covered wagon on one side and a teepee on the other."

While lacking the ruggedness of a real outdoors vacation, a night at the Log Cabin can save the headaches of traffic and dirt roads. "The northwoods calls you to this little cabin complete with wood floors [and] a fireplace (electric)." The winter camper can keep warm in the Northern Lights room. "This cozy igloo holds a 7' round waterbed," brochures say, as well as "a large tiled whirlpool surrounded by mirrors."

Other favorite fantasy rooms include the Sherwood Forest, with beds "up in the trees," and the Treehouse suite: "For the swinger, this suite features a queen size bed suspended from four sturdy oaks."

While the Fantasuites may be a chain, the imagination and audacity involved are impressive. Tours of the rooms run at 3:00 P.M. every Saturday and Sunday so lovers can choose the right room for the perfect romantic tryst.

Quality Inn "Fantasuite Hotel," 250 North River Ridge Circle, (952) 890-9550 or 1-800-666-7829. From the Twin Cities, take I-35W south to Highway 13; the hotel is northeast of the intersection. Go east on Highway 13 until the first stoplight. Turn left and follow the "lodging" signs.

Calumet

Hill Annex Mine

The Open Pit Mine Tour

"**P**ut on good solid shoes," warns the guide. "We're going down five hundred feet into the pit, and there's a lot of red dust down there." Rust red because of the huge quantity of iron still in the crater.

Tours to the bottom of this state park begin in front of the museum

Tourists have replaced the miners on this replica bus, but occasional fossil hunts uncover prehistoric beasts from the time when this area was all ocean bottom.

45

with displays of a chemistry lab, a bunkhouse, and a one-room school. The classic old bus picks up prospectors, and the bus driver is quick to point out "The Big Scoop"—the end of the shovel that could pick up twelve tons of ore with each swoop into the earth. So big that a man could easily stand inside it—or camp in it for that matter!

Miners began digging in 1903 and didn't quit until 1978, when they ran out of good ore. The Department of Natural Resources (DNR) now runs the "Only intact natural iron ore mine in the world that visitors can tour." The hour-and-a-half tour into the 640-acre pit teaches how to process ore and how to separate the iron from the rock. By the end of the trip, visitors feel like real miners, since their pants and heavy shoes are covered with red dust.

Hill Annex Mine, (218) 247-7215 or 1-800-766-6000. Turn north off Highway 169 at the Calumet exit and drive through the town. The mine is just north of Calumet. Summer only.

Chisholm

Ironworld Discovery Center

The Concentrator, the Agglomerator, and the Pelletizer

On the edge of the enormous Glen Open Pit Mine is Ironworld, advertised as having all "The sights, sounds, tastes and smells of the historic Iron Range." Guides in old-time costumes greet guests at the 1915 trolley depot, and a 1920s-era electric trolley circles the 2.5 mile man-made canyon on the "Mesabi Railway." The conductor of the yellow and red train tells stories of the sleeping Ojibwe giant named "Mesabi," whose backbone makes up the huge veins of metal under northern Minnesota.

Check out the yellow "original mobile home" with no basement, so it could be easily transferred when more iron was discovered underneath. Since houses were often moved on a daily basis, miners had trouble finding their way home. What's more, men would come up so dirty from the mines that their own families often couldn't recognize them. To end the tour on an up note, the "Freight Shack Theater" has a sing-along, with Casey playing the banjo and Gloria singing songs in Swedish.

The highlight for kids is definitely Pellet Pete's 19-Hole Mini-Golf Course. As the brochures say, "Each hole of the course tells about a step of the mining process from exploration to shipping. It's educational and fun!" The putting greens have names like "Open Pits," "Iron into Steel," "Ore Dumps," "Pelletizing," and "The Loading Dock," with displays explaining that particular step of the mining process. The "Crushing" hole comes complete with a mini–antique freight car, and the "Blasting" section has a mini–TNT detonator to help kids envision the explosions.

After the kids have putted through the Iron Range, it's time to "Navigate the Great Lakes." Remote-controlled iron ore boats sail on a little pond with a mini–Port of Duluth lift bridge and a lighthouse made to look like Split Rock.

When foreign-exchange students stay in Chisholm, locals supposedly bring them to humbly bow before the sacred Iron Man statue.

A stroll through the grounds of Ironworld reveals a series of houses that were built in the area in the past, such as an Ojibwe teepee, a pioneer homestead, a trapper's cabin, a Finnish Sami Camp, and a Norwegian Stubur house with a sod roof and rosemaling inside.

The main goal of the $8.5 million Ironworld is to recognize all the different ethnic groups that came from forty-three different countries to the Iron Range. Ethnic festivals such as "Festival Finlandia," "All Slav Day," and "Festa Italiana" are regular occurrences. The highlight, however, is International Polkafest, which runs for four days at the end of June with thirty top polka bands. The Minnesota Office of Tourism designated it one of the top twenty-five annual entertainment events, although acts usually close down by 9:00 P.M. every night to start bright and early the next day. The world's first two-step musical and mystery, "Evelyn and the Polka King," was staged here, enticing audiences with "a five-piece polka band, a missing daughter, and stolen money," according to the show's program.

Ironworld is hard to miss on the lunar landscape of the Iron Range since the third largest freestanding memorial in the United States signals the turn along Highway 169. Contrary to popular belief, the eighty-one-foot tall "Iron Man" statue was inspired by Veda Ponikvar's poem "Yes, the Iron Man Lives!" not Ozzy Osborne's heavy metal anthem. If you somehow bypass the statue, the kids won't miss the signs for the amusement park about iron.

Ironworld Discovery Center, (218) 254-3321 or 1-800-372-6437. From Hibbing, head north to Chisholm on Highway 169. Ironworld is just southeast of the highway with large signage. Summer only for amusement park.

While in the Area

"The concentrator. The agglomerator. The pelletizer. These terms may be completely foreign to you now, but after a tour of one of Minnesota's operating taconite plants you'll be using them as knowledgeably as an Iron Range miner," reads a brochure for the Minnesota Museum of Mining, right down the road from Ironworld.

Inside, displays give the facts about Minnesota's iron ore production. Did you know nearly 75 percent of the United States' iron comes from Minnesota, making it 4.4 percent of world production? Replicas of an underground mine give you an idea of past working conditions, then imagine sleeping on the floor in shifts afterward!

At the Minnesota Museum of Mining, you can put on a hard hat and walk into a simulated mine shaft that shows tourists the hardships faced by iron ore miners. Above ground, old machinery lies dormant in the yard, dwarfing visitors.

The castle-like entrance to the museum lies amidst a yard filled with enormous old machinery and railcars from the mines. You'll even find Paul Bunyan's marble on the grounds.

Minnesota Museum of Mining, Highway 169 (at the end of Main Street), (218) 254-5543 or (218) 254-7158. Turn north off Highway 169 toward downtown, then take the first left toward the town park and the Air National Guard base. The museum is to the left of the park.

Cloquet

Frank Lloyd Wright Gas Station
Fill 'er Up with Modernism

While it may seem odd that one of America's most famous architects designed something as ordinary as a gas station, Frank
Lloyd Wright was actually a strong advocate of the automobile and
suburbanization. "In our present gasoline service station you may see
a crude beginning to such important advance decentralization. . . .
Wherever service stations are located naturally these so often ugly and
seemingly insignificant features will survive and expand," said Wright
in 1930.

The R. W. Lindholm Service Station wasn't constructed until 1956,
however, the same boom year that saw eighteen other Wright buildings
rise, including the Solomon R. Guggenheim Museum in New York. He
had already designed the Lindholms' house Mäntylä in Cloquet four
years earlier, so for their gas station, the family used one of Wright's
old designs from his futuristic plans of "Broadacre City."

The Lindholm Service Station was the only part of Wright's
"Broadacre" plans that was ever realized, but postwar suburbanization proved his prophecies correct. "Broadacre City" added "car-
ports" onto "Usonian" homes, usually placing them on the side of the
house as a pedestal for the car. This revolutionary idea broke from the
Victorian trend of putting the garage/stable behind the building to
avoid the stench of the horses' road apples wafting onto the front
porch and spoiling teatime.

"We shall solve the city problems by leaving the city," declared
Henry Ford in his motorized march to colonize suburbia. Wright
probably agreed with this sentiment to an extent, but he also waxed
poetic about redesigning American cities like Chicago with wide boule-
vards, so cars could zip in and out without any traffic.

"Every woman, man, and child in America is entitled to own an
acre of ground as long as they live on it or use it, and every man at least

You can still fill 'er up at Cloquet's Prairie School gas station at the corner of Highways 33 and 45, shown here in 1963.

owning his own car," Wright said, according to John Sergeant in *Frank Lloyd Wright's Usonian Houses.*

At the 1939 World's Fair in New York, the General Motors display was awash with highway propaganda, declaring, "If we are to have full use of automobiles, cities must be remade. . . . A waiting industry that will do wonders for prosperity will spring up when we revamp our cities and make it safe, convenient, pleasant and easy to use a car on city streets." Frank Lloyd Wright concurred, envisioning elevated sidewalks so cars could steer right up to storefronts and peer in the windows at the latest fashions. As a compromise, urban centers across the country trimmed their sidewalks back to half their width.

Frank Lloyd Wright's gas station may be a departure from most of his buildings, but the grace of his pen can be seen in the cantilevered roof stretching over the pumps, as though suspended in midair. While cars are being tuned on the lift, customers can kick back in the waiting lounge upstairs. Wright's 1956 station stands as a remembrance of things fast and the push for continual acceleration, modernization, and, of course, endless highways.

Frank Lloyd Wright Gas Station, 202 Cloquet Avenue, (218) 879-2279. From I-35, take Highway 33 (exit 237) straight into Cloquet. Before crossing the river, look for the gas station on the right on the corner of Cloquet Avenue (Highway 45).

While in the Area

Jessica Lange hails from Cloquet, but rather than raising a statue of King Kong in her honor, the town decided to delve further into its past

Standing in Dunlap Island Park, Cloquet's famous French-Canadian statue of the World's Largest Voyageur towers above the river that was once a highway for the fur trade.

and pay tribute to the French-Canadian traders. As a bicentennial project, "The World's Largest Voyageur" was erected on an island in the St. Louis River with a little wooden fort next to it that doubles as an amphitheater during the summer months. Logging chic runs rampant during Lumberjack Days at the beginning of July, when voyageur acts perform to charm the tots.

Cold Spring

Grasshopper Chapel

Miraculous Salvation from an Insect Swarm

"It gradually darkened. The men hastily went out to see if anything should be brought in before the storm," said one of the survivors of the spring of 1876. "What a sight when we opened the door! The sky darkened by myriads of grasshoppers and no green thing could be seen."

A hundred grasshoppers would attack a single stack of wheat, eat

Grasshoppers bow like praying mantises to the Virgin at the "Grasshopper Chapel," where pilgrims flocked to beseech Mary for a respite from the insect plagues.

55

everything, and move on to the next. Clothes were eaten right off the lines, leaving only the buttons on the ground. Some cattle were even killed from blood poisoning.

To try to keep the insects at bay, people dug ditches around their fields and lit huge fires. Farmers made "hopperdozers" and dragged sheets of metal sopped down with tar across their fields. Once the metal was inundated, they'd toss a match onto it, let it burn down, and "harvest" some more grasshoppers.

According to the state entomologist, two-thirds of the state was covered with grasshopper eggs ready to hatch in the spring of 1877. Minnesotans called upon their governor, John S. Pillsbury, to do something to prevent another onset of the plague.

With what became known as "Pillsbury's Best"—in a parody of the brand of flour—he declared a statewide "Day of Prayer." All businesses were to be closed on April 26th, 1877, for "a day of fasting, humiliation and prayer in view of the threatened continuation of the grasshopper scourge," according to his gubernatorial proclamation.

The Liberal League assailed the governor: "We hold that this belief in the power of prayer is palpably untrue, its influence pernicious, and in this day a marked discredit to the intelligence of Minnesotans. From the beginning down to this day, outside of so-called Sacred History, there is not one well-authorized instance of such prayer having been answered, not one."

Father Leo Winter agreed with the governor that the plague was a punishment sent by God. He pledged to build a little chapel near Cold Spring where sinners could repent in hopes of staving off another pestilence.

Reporters from around the country came to Minnesota for this day of prayer; all bars and stores were closed as residents stayed home or went to church.

Then, a miracle happened. "Entomologists did not prophesy it. Editors did not expect it. Statesmen dared not hope for it. Infidels railed at the bare idea of it," wrote an elated New York journalist. A wintry rain appeared out of nowhere and rained down ice on the eggs, freezing most of the grasshoppers just as they were hatching.

Father Winter was not surprised. "It must be reported," he said, "that as soon as the promise was made and building begun, the grasshoppers departed by and by." The Assumption Chapel, or Grasshopper Chapel, was soon finished for Minnesotans to pledge their eternal gratitude for the favor. Annual pilgrimages were made to the little wooden chapel, with the penitents climbing the steep hill either barefoot or on their knees, saying a prayer at each step of the way.

In 1894, a tornado blew the church into the trees, scattering its lumber around the hill. The angry twister then headed north, ripping down the church at Jacob's Prairie and putting a sizable dent in St. John's Abbey.

In 1951, the Assumption Chapel was replaced by one made of beautiful local granite, with kneeling grasshoppers carved at the feet of the Virgin Mary above the door. Outside the chapel under an oak grove is the way of the cross, with stations leading to the small stone chapel perched on the hill.

The interior walls of polished agate and carnelian along with the beautiful stained-glass windows complement the rough pink-grey granite. Ironically, a huge swarm of wasps has recently moved into the eaves of the church, but there hasn't been a grasshopper plague in Minnesota since 1877.

Grasshopper Chapel. Take Highway 23 east out of Cold Spring past the quarry. Turn right on Chapel Street, then left on Pilgrimage Road.

While in the Area

The crystal clear water of Cold Spring made it the perfect place to set up Gluek's Brewery. So perfect, in fact, that Jimmy Carter's brother decided to have his famous Billy Beer brewed here. "All beer is good," proclaimed the tour guide at the brewery when asked if he prefers foreign or domestic beer.

Gluek Brewing Company, 219 Red River Avenue North, (320) 685-8686.

Crosby

Nordic Inn Medieval B & B
Viking Valhalla

"**L**ooking for a quiet weekend?" asks the brochure for the Nordic Inn. "Don't look here! We celebrate the three Rs: Rowdy, Robust, and Romantic."

Rick Schmidthuber says he never laughed at his well-paying, boring job. He changed his name to Steinarr Elmerson and invested all his time and money renovating a little 1909 church in a quiet Crosby neighborhood. He then opened a B & B, which in his book translates as "Brew-n-Bed."

A chainsaw sculpture of Thor, the Viking God of Thunder, stubbornly guards the door. The antler door handles don't budge, and pounding on the huge wooden doors gets no response. Pull the enormous chain to sound a basso profundo bullhorn deep inside, however, and Elmerson greets you in chain mail and a horned helmet. Remember the password?

The armor-clad manager offers a slice of birch or cedar wood for your soap, and Viking outfits complete the experience. The B & B has only five rooms, decked out in medieval style with beds in boats.

Elmerson's passion for the modern Vikings, i.e., the football team, shows up in "The Locker Room." Artificial turf is underfoot and Viking logos are everywhere. Closets are replaced with metal sports lockers, and football goalposts make up the suggestive headboards of the bed. The only place that's lacking a Viking symbol is the urinal, which has a Green Bay Packers logo for a target.

Dinner is done Nordic style with "Viking portions!" Lots of potatoes and other root vegetables round out the meat and fish, but no utensils are allowed, except for an old-style dull knife. Napkins are discouraged until the end of the meal. "When in Oslo. . . ."

After supper, the fun begins. What was a church sanctuary now has

In a quiet neighborhood in Crosby, the Nordic Thor, god of chainsaw sculptures, guards the once-holy church.

huge stained-glass windows of Odin, King of the Gods, basking in the sun of Valhalla. Under Odin's Scandinavian heaven is a large bar with heavy stools carved from tree trunks. While sipping one of Elmerson's hardy brews, you can choose one of three different interactive dinner

Suffering sea serpents! Locals fib about sea creatures swimming around in Serpent Lake, nibbling at toddlers' toes.

theaters, in which local improv actors don Viking garb for a play with you, the guest, as the butt of the jokes.

After a brief hop in the whirlpool in a fiberglass cave, it's time for bed in a boat. Give the front desk a call if you need a 7:00 A.M. wake-up call, but be prepared for a jolt when a loud Viking horn springs you out of bed.

Just south of Crosby lies tiny Deerwood, whose name derives from an early settler's having seen a large buck jumping over a log on this spot.

Elmerson has realized his goal of laughing at work, but now he hopes to transform a few other churches in the state into Nordic Inns. He told the *Star Tribune* in 1997: "There's one in Duluth that's three blocks from Leif Erickson Park. Hey, you gotta dream."

Nordic Inn Medieval B & B, 210 First Avenue NW, (218) 546-8299. From Brainerd, go northeast on Highway 210 to Crosby.

While in the Area

If you're done lugging in walleyes on the area lakes, stop at the Croft Mine Historical Park in Crosby and gawk at the rock that is almost a ton of copper. Weighing 1,884 pounds, or "the equivalent of 310,000 pennies," the mineral was found in 1921 and has been on display ever since.

When you've seen enough of the rock, "experience a simulated mine shaft ride in the old shaft cage, which offers a realistic 'journey' into the depths of the mine," according to the museum brochure. "The sounds of ore drills add to the unique adventure," it says.

The Cuyuna Range Historical Society Museum in the old train depot has old photos and mining equipment from the Cuyuna mine—named for owner Cuyler Adams and his dog Una. Minerals are no longer excavated, possibly because of a ghostly presence.

On February 5, 1924, while workers were busy mining for manganiferous ore in the Milford Mine, a shaft was dug too close to the bottom of Foley's Lake. With a flood of water rushing in, miner Clinton Harris rang the warning bell frantically to alert the upper levels, rather than escaping himself. In fifteen minutes the entire mine was submerged, leaving forty-one dead and only seven survivors. Harris's bell continued to sound for five hours afterward. When the mine was drained a few months later, a pair of excavators found Clinton Harris's body grasping the ladder, staring blank-eyed toward the surface. The miners raced to the surface and refused to go back.

Cuyuna Range Historical Society Museum, 101 First Street NE, (218) 546-6178. Croft Mine Historical Park, Second Avenue East and Spalj Drive, (218) 546-5625 or (218) 546-5466. Summer only.

Darwin

World's Largest Ball of Twine

Man's Dream Realized

Francis Johnson was obsessed. He collected anything that caught his fancy, including five thousand pencils, more than two hundred feed caps, wooden ice cream buckets, padlocks, and pliers. Residents of Darwin thought him a little odd, especially when he painted his cupola blue and yellow in a bout of Swedish patriotism. Only later would locals realize that he was shaping the identity of the entire town.

His secret project was a string collection he'd begun in March 1950. He dutifully wrapped twine for four hours every day. Soon, his hobby wouldn't fit in the house anymore, so he rolled it out to the shed, where he used a railroad jack to continue to wind twine in one continuous string. From the blue and yellow cupola, he brought it into his barn, where he hooked up a crane to elevate the ball for proper wrapping.

At this point, people began to take notice of Johnson's masterpiece. A representative from *The Guinness Book of Records* snapped a photo and the ball of twine took its place in the annals of history, outshining the man with the beard of bees and the guy with the longest fingernails. Johnson had done it, but he didn't stop there. He kept winding and winding until the ball reached twelve feet in diameter and weighed eleven tons.

While Johnson was basking in the limelight, Frank Stoeber of Cawker, Kansas, was itching with envy. He had been working on a twine ball of his own for years with no recognition. Thinking that Johnson was resting on his laurels, Stoeber wound 1.6 million feet of baler twine night and day. Victory was in sight as his ball reached eleven feet in diameter, then he had a tragic heart attack and died in 1974.

Cawker, Kansas, humbly conceded victory to Darwin, Minnesota, but they built a shelter for the ball in the town square. Every year, residents of Cawker gather at the Twine-a-thon festival and add more string to the ball in tribute to Frank Stoeber. Although the ball has

The life's work of eccentric Francis Johnson put Darwin on the map. The town honors his twelve-foot-wide, eleven-ton creation every year during Twine Ball Days.

surpassed forty feet in diameter, Johnson's magnum opus still claims the title of "World's Largest Ball of Twine by a Single Person."

In 1989, Johnson passed away after having wrapped twine for thirty-nine years. The battle of the biggest, however, marched on.

In 1992, Ripley's Believe It or Not asked Darwin if it could have the ball for its museum. The tiny town appreciated the offer, but flatly refused to let its homespun oddity be shipped away. Ripley's was undaunted and turned to Mr. J. P. Payne from Mountain Springs, Texas, to make one that ended up measuring thirteen feet, two and a half inches. "It's probably bigger, but doesn't weigh as much, it's not of twine and not done by one person," according to the woman at the "Twine Ball Souvenir Shack" in Darwin. She laments these other copycat balls since "They took us out of Guinness."

In between selling tickets to the annual chicken dinner, she graciously shows photos of Weird Al Yankovic's visit after he wrote a song about the ball of twine. "It's a good song," she says. "Some of the songs aren't so nice on that channel, but his was great. He even projected the twine ball on the screen behind him!"

The twine ball has been moved from Johnson's front yard into a Plexiglas silo in the main square of downtown (where it can dry out a little, since it was getting a little pungent). Darwin has finally embraced Johnson's dream as the town symbol, and "Twine Ball Days" are celebrated every year. The ball of twine even has its own mailbox.

World's Largest Ball of Twine by a Single Person. From Highway 12, turn south into Darwin. The twine ball is on the left in a little park.

While in the Area

After taking photos of the string that made Guinness, stop in at The Ball of Twine Inn across the street, which serves up "real potatoes and homemade bread." Another of Francis Johnson's obsessions is on display on the wall: pliers. An eight-foot-long pair of pliers opens up into twenty-six more pliers in a Rubik's Cube–style puzzle.

Old Depot Railroad Museum in Dassel

"They came first by horseback and ox cart, letting the moon and stars guide them. Then the railroad lines stretched across the state, bringing new settlers by the thousands," says the brochure for the Old Depot Railroad Museum in Dassel.

The miniature train out front shows motorists passing on Highway 12 the transportation that originally brought settlers from the Twin Cities to western Minnesota. Climb on a caboose from 1922 to get a feel for life on the rails, with a little stove, desk, and toilet with a hole onto the tracks below.

Mannequins wait patiently in the entrance room of "The Depot That Time Forgot." Inside the little railroad station, which was moved west from Cokato, is a collection of old railroad paraphernalia and a railroad scooter that could be pedaled on top of the train tracks—as long as no choo-choos were in sight.

Old Depot Railroad Museum, 651 Highway 12, (320) 275-3876. The museum is just west of downtown Dassel on the way to the twine ball in Darwin. Summer only.

Delano

Blue-Eyed Chicken

"Famous across the Nation"

O n the road to the World's Largest Ball of Twine stands a huge red and white, blue-eyed chicken in front of a Tom Thumb Superette. The rooster was built in 1990 by F.A.S.T. (Fiberglass Animals, Shapes, and Trademarks) for "Chicken John" to advertise his famous fried

Delano's rooster calls Highway 12 road workers in for some of Chicken John's cooking or one of Flippin' Bill's burgers.

chicken. "Truckers across the nation know about the chicken," according to Dawn, the assistant manager at the store, where the chicken is sold.

Chicken John sold out to his brother, "Flippin' Bill," who decided to add his famous "Bill's Burgers" to the menu. "We don't have a big burger statue, so we just kept the chicken," Dawn notes. But are the burgers as good as the chicken? "You bet! Flippin' Bill makes the best burgers around!"

Chicken John's influence lives on, though, in the black chicken tracks that mark the floor of the convenience store leading to the tasty fried chicken.

Chicken John's Blue-Eyed Chicken. Take Highway 12 just east of downtown Delano and look for the Tom Thumb.

While in the Area

The "Peppermint Twist" Drive-In Restaurant is worth a stop, mostly to see the Teddy Bear Park erected in 1999. Someone with a jigsaw, a lot of lumber, and a teddy bear template created a kid's playground featuring a mini-putt golf course where every hole is around a teddy bear silhouette.

Duluth

Glensheen Mansion

Murder Estate

This is a tale of greed, murder, and bigamy. The setting is one of the largest houses in Duluth with the waves of Lake Superior persistently pounding on the front lawn. Enthralled with wealth and perhaps the closest thing Minnesota has to royalty, tourists wander in and out of the chateau, by the fountains, and through the flower gardens, looking out on the ships navigating the lake.

The mansion is on the National Register of Historic Places and has been run as a museum by the University of Minnesota since 1979. The guides, however, are told not to reveal the dark history of this palace.

Elisabeth Congdon had just returned home from her summer estate in northern Wisconsin. Her house was the enormous Glensheen mansion built by her father, iron baron Chester Congdon, in 1905. Elisabeth inherited her family's millions, making her one of the richest women in the state. She never married, but her desire for children led her to adopt two daughters. One of her daughters led a quiet life; the other, Marjorie, didn't.

Having grown up in Glensheen, Marjorie continued to lust for luxury far beyond her means after she moved away from Duluth. She imagined that her elderly mother's will would probably split the family fortune between the two sisters, so she wasn't afraid of owing a little money in the meantime.

By the early 1970s, Marjorie and her husband, Roger Caldwell, were deep in debt. Roger asked Elisabeth's trustees for a loan, but was denied.

At eighty-three years old, Elisabeth didn't venture out much since she was partially paralyzed, so her Wisconsin trip had tired her out. Her nurse helped her get into bed that night of June 26, 1977. Elisabeth was never to see daylight again.

A man had been hiding in the cemetery near the mansion, waiting for the lights to go out. He then hopped up onto the back patio, quietly broke the window of the billiard room, and sneaked into the mansion. He seemed to know his way around the building fairly well, but may have been drunk since the burglary job was awkward at best.

He quietly stepped upstairs. Then a flashlight blinded the burglar as the night nurse shrieked. He grabbed her, threw her on the steps, and bludgeoned her with a long brass candelabra (Colonel Mustard with the candlestick!). She lay motionless on the ground, bleeding to death, with strands of his hair clutched in her fist.

The killer rushed into Elisabeth's room, took a pink satin pillow from the bed, and jammed it over her sleeping face. She struggled as best she could, but was dead within five minutes.

Tourists heading up the North Shore should stop at Glensheen Mansion to tour the site of a millionaire murder mystery worthy of an Agatha Christie novel.

The blood from the nurse was still all over the murderer's hands, so he wiped them off on the sheets and his shirt. He dug clumsily through Elisabeth's dresser drawers, filling a bag with her jewelry. He looked back at the body and noticed her gleaming rings. He pried them off the dead woman's hands, one by one.

His job done, he rushed down the steps, jumped over the poor nurse, and got into his car parked nearby. With his booty in hand, he drove to the airport in Minneapolis.

The police found the gruesome scene the next day, and the task of investigating fell into the lap of the "Duluth Sleuth," Chief Ernie Grams. The media hounded him for the real story, but the stoic Grams merely referred to it as a simple burglary gone awry. Behind the scenes, the investigation was going full speed. Mounting evidence led to the arrest of Elisabeth's son-in-law, Roger Caldwell, in Colorado nine days later.

Publicity compelled the judge to move the trial to Brainerd. On July 8, 1978, Roger was convicted of double murder and handed two consecutive life sentences.

A few days after the sentencing, prosecutors charged Marjorie with conspiring with Roger to kill her mother to speed up the inheritance. She was later acquitted of all charges, and the jury even invited her to a party after the trial in sympathy.

Marjorie ended up inheriting more than a quarter of the family trust. Her new life began with a wedding in North Dakota to Wallace Hagen, but somehow she forgot to file for a divorce from Roger. A year and a half later, the state of North Dakota filed bigamy charges against her that would be carried out if she returned to that state.

Due to new evidence at Marjorie's trial, Roger was released in 1982. To avoid another lengthy trial, a plea bargain was reached in which Roger pleaded guilty to second-degree murder, but was set free based on time served.

Roger moved home to Pennsylvania to start over, but nobody wanted to hire a convicted murderer. "I'm so disenchanted with the hand I've been dealt, but there's not a thing I can do about it," he told Joe Kimball in *Secrets of the Congdon Mansion*. His bleak existence led him to slit his wrists. He died in 1988, still claiming he'd never killed Elisabeth and her nurse.

Marjorie never bothered to get divorced from Roger, even after the bigamy charges, perhaps because she was already in court battling three counts of arson. Before serving time for one of her convictions in 1992, she was allowed by the judge to stop home to gather her things.

The next day when officials came to fetch her, they found her new husband Wally dead of an overdose. Marjorie was acquitted of murder charges, but remains behind bars for arson.

For more information, read Joe Kimball's *Secrets of the Congdon Mansion*, which is not available in the Glensheen gift shop.

Following the sordid events at Glensheen, a play called "Keep Tightly Closed in a Cool, Dry Place" was written about this real-life murder mystery. More disturbing still was the 1972 movie, "You'll Like My Mother," filmed in the Glensheen Mansion before the murders and re-played at a Duluth cinema following the crimes. In an eerie foreshadowing, the plot features a young woman visiting her mother-in-law in the huge family home, but somebody is impersonating the elder lady since she has already been murdered.

Glensheen Mansion, 3300 London Road, (218) 724-8864 or 1-888-454-GLEN. Drive five miles east of downtown on Highway 61, and look for it on the lake side of the road. Extended summer hours; from November through April, open Friday, Saturday, and Sunday only, 11:00 A.M. to 2:00 P.M.

Duluth

William A. Irvin Steamer
The Big Tour

The *William A. Irvin* tour is all about size. "See the immense cargo compartments," boasts the brochure. Indeed they are impressive, big enough to fill two hundred rail cars, which translates into 14,000 tons of cargo. To move this tonnage, 1.2 tons of coal were burned each hour to spin the two 1,000 horsepower turbine engines. Sailors didn't have to worry about getting cold on the frigid lake since the motor room could reach up to 115° Fahrenheit when the ship topped out at a poky eleven knots.

There's something for everyone here. As the brochure says, "Whether you're interested in a 2,000-horsepower steam turbine engine or delicate antique fixtures, you'll find them all in shipshape!"

As flagship for the U.S. Steel Great Lakes Fleet, the *Irvin* stretched more than two football fields in length and the captain was perched in the pilot's house six stories above the lake. As well as moving tons of iron ore, the steamer doubled as a luxury cruiser, hosting visiting dignitaries.

Captain John J. McDonough recorded the final entry of the captain's log in 1986, after the *Irvin* had sailed for more than forty years: "She was the Queen of the Lakes and so shall remain for the rest of her days." The *William A. Irvin* is now docked, naturally, in the world's largest freshwater port, Duluth.

William A. Irvin Steamer, (218) 722-7876 (summer) and (218) 722-5573 (off-season). From I-35, turn on Canal Park Drive, then take a right on Railroad Street. The ship is at the corner of Harbor Drive on the waterfront, near the Omnimax Theater. Summer only.

Looking from below like a big red building, the *William A. Irvin* was the Great Lakes' Love Boat for a few lucky passengers who were hosted in the luxury quarters of U.S. Steel's flagship. Dwarfed by the *Irvin*, the Lake Superior tugboat, on the other side of the ship, huffed and puffed to pull this clumsy carrier in and out of port.

While in the Area

To ride one of these huge ships and see "The City in a Rock Garden" from the water, call up Vista Fleet Harbor Cruises at (218) 722-6218. Finally all the cars will have to wait for you, since the ships pass under the lift bridge twice.

Duluth

World's Largest Aerial Lift Bridge

Elevator to the Heavens

Follow the sounds of the squawking seagulls to the world's largest aerial lift bridge, visible from nearly any high point in town. The traffic halts as each new barge rolls into Duluth harbor and the middle section of this iron bridge rises into the sky. After a few minutes, cars sputter across the metal grates of the bridge out to Park Point and its beautiful sand beach along the south shore of Lake Superior. No wonder the lift bridge has become the symbol of Duluth.

Canal Park at the foot of the bridge is ground zero for Duluth tourism. Cappuccino cafés, Duluth Packs, and Grandma's ever-expanding restaurant are favorite hot spots on the small peninsula overlooking Lake Superior, the world's largest freshwater lake.

Displays at the Lake Superior Maritime Visitors' Center next to the bridge in Canal Park explain that this enormous lake contains 20 percent of the world's freshwater. A lesser known fact is that Russia's Lake Baikal holds double the amount of water. The usual retort is that Lake Baikal covers only 12,500 square miles, whereas Superior is nearly triple the area at 31,700 square miles. The Maritime Center is operated by the U.S. Army Corps of Engineers and features reconstructed ship cabins and tours inside a huge steam engine.

World's Largest Aerial Lift Bridge, Canal Park, and Lake Superior Maritime Visitors' Center, (218) 727-2497. From I-35, turn on Canal Park Drive. The road dead-ends at the visitors' center, which is open summer only.

While in the Area

If the waves make you queasy, you can hop on the vintage trains of the Lake Superior & Mississippi Railroad Company for a ninety-minute

Many tragic stories tell about people getting stuck or cut or jumping from the world's largest aerial lift bridge. These urban legends are probably created by bored motorists with vivid imaginations who picture grotesque scenes while waiting for the bridge to come back down.

trip along the St. Louis River. Call (218) 624-7549 or (218) 727-8025 in the summer.

Another favorite is the all-you-can-eat "Pizza Train," also known as the North Shore Scenic Railroad, with trips from ninety minutes to six hours up the coast of Lake Superior. The longest ride stops in Two Harbors for a two-hour layover (probably to give guests a chance to see the famous Sandpaper Museum). Trains depart from the Old Depot at 506 West Michigan Street. Call (218) 722-1273.

Embarrass

The Nation's Cold Spot
"Freeze Yer Gizzard"

Chainsaw statues of Finnish farmers guard the famous weather station in Embarrass, a town that claims to be the coldest spot in the lower forty-eight states. With an average temperature of 34.4° in Embarrass, it's no wonder all those Finns like to sweat in the sauna.

The coldest state temperatures on record, however, were set by other northern Minnesota communities. On February 9, 1899, Leech Lake Dam hit –59°, a record that was tied on February 16, 1903, at the nearby Pokegama Dam. This second claim, however, is contested and listed as "suspect" in the record books.

All records were broken on February 2, 1996, when the mercury plummeted to -60° in nearby Tower. For fun and to stave off cabin fever, locals boiled water, then ran outside and heaved it into the air. The steamy liquid crackled and froze instantly, tumbling to the ground as ice crystals. In this area, where global warming is a welcome trend, only fools turn off their cars when stopping at the bar. Many cars are left going all night long, lest little fires have to be started beneath the engines to resuscitate the dead.

International Falls, nicknamed "Frostbite Falls" by Rocky and Bullwinkle, has raised a twenty-two-foot-high thermometer—as if residents need to be reminded they're living in "The Nation's Icebox." Standing in Smokey the Bear Park, the digital gauge records the average temp at a frosty 36.8°. Unfortunately, International Falls can't quite claim to have "The World's Largest Thermometer," since California mounted a gargantuan one in the Mojave Desert.

As part of Icebox Days at the end of January, outdoor chess matches test which team can suffer the most frostbite. Other chilly favorites are the "Freeze Yer Gizzard Blizzard Run," the "Sleet Feet Obstacle Course," the "Frostbite Falls Frozen Foot Broomball Tournament," and curling, with jam pails substituted for the hefty stones. To top it off,

The famous weather center in Embarrass is ground zero for the coldest
temperatures in the lower forty-eight states. In 1996, Tower bottomed out
at -60°, but Embarrass still claims the coldest average temp of 34.4°.

everyone gathers for a frigid beach party to prove they're not afraid of Jack Frost. Would they do that in California?

While in the Area

The name *Embarrass* has sparked much speculation. Local Finns claim it stems from Father Du Poisson (literally "of the fish"), a Frenchman who called the river flowing through town *embara,* or "obstacle," in the 1790s. In his letters he warned fellow voyageurs to avoid the Embara River, except during years of high water.

Embarrass isn't ashamed of its past. Tours of old Finnish log cabins leave from near the Four Corners Café daily at 10:00 A.M. and 2:00 P.M. and tour the Finnish farm on the north side of town, as well as various houses in the area. Guests can get some shut-eye at a 1901 Finnish homestead, as well as a special farm-style breakfast.

Heritage Homestead Tours. Meet at the Visitor Center at Highway 135 and County Road 21. Call (218) 984-2106 or (218) 984-2672.

Finnish Heritage Homestead Bed & Breakfast, 4776 Waisanen Road, (218) 984-3318.

Eveleth

U.S. Hockey Hall of Fame
World's Largest Hockey Stick

Driving on Highway 53 through the Iron Range, you can see the U.S. Hockey Hall of Fame standing high on a hill. While northern Minnesota may seem like an odd spot for such an important national monument, brochures assert that "no other town of Eveleth's size in the country has contributed so much to the sport of ice hockey."

The town formed its first hockey team in 1902. In 1956, four members of the Olympic Hockey Team hailed from Eveleth. Local legends include Frank Brimsek and John Mariucci, both of whom made it into that other Hockey Hall of Fame in Toronto. Since 1972, Eveleth has called itself "The Hockey Capital of the United States."

The Hall of Fame also declares that "no other state has contributed more than Minnesota" to hockey. Minnesota has more professional and Olympic players than any other state, and St. Paul native Charles Schulz is even in the Hall of Fame, a testament to his love of the sport and to Snoopy's toothless grin—proof positive that he's a hockey player.

Visitors can't help but whistle "I Wanna Drive a Zamboni" by the Gear Daddies as they see the fourth ice machine ever built in the front entrance. The fancy modern Zambonis evolved from these early four-wheel-drive Jeeps with attached ice shavers.

The Great Hall features a display dedicated to the U.S. gold medal teams in 1960 and 1980. You can see a dangerous-looking view of the game through the goalie's mask.

On the second floor, a time-tunnel display chronicles the dawn of the sport in 478 B.C. as a form of ice polo all the way through the full-contact hockey of modern times. The origin of the term *hat trick* is revealed as a cricket custom in which the bowler is given a hat if he hits three wickets in a row.

After seeing all these displays of players in action, the highlight of the museum is inevitably the ice rink, where you can get your hands on a hockey stick to test your skill. Although the sign warns "No Slap-shots," it's hard to resist. Obviously the same enticement has tempted other Gretsky wannabes, since there are black marks from hockey pucks everywhere.

A stop in downtown Eveleth is called for afterward to salute the World's Largest Hockey Stick. Although the stick hasn't made Guinness yet, hopes are high. A giant wooden sculpture of a hockey stick stands in Canada, but locals are quick to point out that it isn't a real hockey stick. Rumor has it that Guinness just laughed when the Canadian town tried to make the book of records.

The Eveleth stick was constructed with the help of the Christian Brothers hockey stick factory in Warroad. The 107-foot-long stick took thirty laminations to make it regulation and blocked traffic for four hours as a truck hauled it in September 1995 to its destination on the

Ready for the face-off! The World's Largest Hockey Stick stands over downtown Eveleth, just up the road from the U.S. Hockey Hall of Fame.

main street. Across the alley is a huge goalie mural, the obvious target for the stick and its seven-hundred-pound puck. All they need is a big enough player.

U.S. Hockey Hall of Fame, 801 Hat Trick Avenue, (218) 744-5167 or 1-800-443-7825. Follow the signs off of Highway 53.

Excelsior

Minnehaha Streetcar Boat

Raised from the Deep

Far below the waves of Lake Minnetonka lay six steamboats from the early 1900s, like Spanish galleons in freshwater. For more than fifty years they lay hidden at the bottom, visited only by the occasional northern pike. Then one day in 1979, a local diver discovered one boat, the *Minnehaha*, amidst the mud and seaweed of the deep.

The "streetcar boat"—named because of its looks and the connection it had to the streetcar line ending in Excelsior—was raised to the surface. It took $500,000 and 80,000 mostly volunteer hours, but six years later the *Minnehaha* had been restored to its past glory, powered by a nearly identical steam engine dating from 1946.

"Keep your hands outside of the engine. Safety regulations are different today than in 1906," warns the captain, but when you travel on the beautiful *Minnehaha,* you feel like you're a part of old-time Lake Minnetonka, when John Philip Sousa played at the Big Island Dance Pavilion. Imagine buying a fifty-cent round-trip ticket on the streetcar from Minneapolis, connecting with a steamboat in Excelsior, and then touring the lake with stops at Orono, Wayzata, Spring Lake, or maybe a lake cabin (as long as there's a dock). The neighbors complained like mad about the big band music wafting across the lake from the dance hall. Things got even more lively when the Excelsior amusement park opened in 1925 with "The Whip," the "Chair-o-Plane" ride, "The Caterpillar," a Ferris wheel, and the "Electric Flying Skooters."

Thanks to land developer Thomas "The Streetcar Man" Lowry, tracks had been laid in 1905, stretching from White Bear Lake to Excelsior. Lowry bought out the enormous 1,100-room Tonka Bay Hotel and the White House Hotel on Lake Minnetonka, and travelers came from all over the world to enjoy the splendors of the lake—and sometimes to buy some real estate.

By the 1920s, however, the boom had faded. The streetcar boats

Raise the *Minnehaha*! After fifty-four years underwater, the *Minnehaha* streetcar boat was hoisted to the surface and now cruises Lake Minnetonka once again.

were scuttled one by one and sent to rest at the bottom of the lake. The *Minnehaha,* which had been built in 1906, was sunk in 1926 and spent fifty-four years underwater. By 1932, the line to Lake Minnetonka was closed. The dance pavilion was burned to the ground by an arsonist in 1973. The carousel and roller coaster were moved to Valleyfair amusement park and condos were built in their place, blocking the lake view.

The last boat to escape the ax, the *Hopkins,* joined its sisters in 1948. The day before it was scheduled to be sent to its final resting place, someone boarded the *Hopkins* and stole the steering wheel. Today that very wheel adorns the *Minnehaha,* helping the steamboat navigate the waters of Lake Minnetonka and giving passengers an idea of Excelsior's heyday.

Minnehaha Streetcar Boat, 1-800-711-2591. After entering Excelsior, follow Water Street (main street) toward the lake. Tours on the *Minnehaha* leave from the docks at Excelsior Bay at the end of Water Street. Weekends during the summer.

While in the Area

A half-mile stretch of streetcar track has been restored along the old Minneapolis & St. Louis Railroad line. Streetcar #1239 is currently being restored to travel on this line from the old Excelsior depot on Water Street to the dock where the *Minnehaha* Streetcar Boat departs.

For a longer railway trip, hop aboard the Hiawatha Dinner Train in nearby Spring Park for supper on the rails. Call (952) 471-7811.

Fergus Falls

World's Largest Otter

Part Jungle Gym, Part Sculpture

Just about every creature that makes Minnesota its home ends up being idolized in the form of an enormous fiberglass or cement structure hundreds of times its size, like the Fergus Falls otter.

Local schoolteacher-cum-artist Robert Burns built a few other large sculptures around the area, such as an enormous mallard in Wheaton. His masterpiece, however, is the forty-foot-long otter next to Adams Park, which can be climbed on by anyone who can get up on his back.

Inspired by this new symbol of Fergus Falls's status as the county seat of Otter Tail County, miniature replicas of the sculpture popped up along Main Street. A few years later, the city of Chicago plagiarized Fergus's idea by placing artist-designed cows along the streets of the windy city.

Local teenagers viewed this line-up of otters as their canvas, spray painting them all the colors of the rainbow. Some even brought their heads home on a platter, perhaps in reference to John the Baptist's noggin offered to Salomé. "Everyone was doing it that summer," said a local teen who asked to go unnamed. "I think Fergus tried to put out new otters the next year, but then gave up."

Even so, the large otter is still the symbol of Fergus Falls, and the envy of nearby towns. When a worker at the local convenience store was asked his opinion of the otter, he called it a "rat, or weasel, or whatever it is." The woman working with him noted, "Oh, don't listen to him, he's just jealous since he's from Alexandria. All they have there is an old Viking rock."

World's Largest Otter. Take the Highway 210 exit north off of I-94. Turn left on Pebble Lake Road and the otter will appear soon after in Adams Park.

Just about every native creature in Minnesota is idolized in the form of a fiberglass structure hundreds of times its size, like this Fergus Falls otter.

While in the Area

As you enter Fergus from the other direction off of exit 54, look for the huge Canada goose sculpture in front of the Otter Tail County Historical Museum on Lincoln Avenue.

Frazee

World's Largest Turkey
Tons of Roast Meat

With eyes always open, watching anxiously, Big Tom stands twenty-two feet high on the hill above the town of Frazee. Tom is "The World's Largest Turkey" and he has good reason to be nervous, even when it's nowhere near November.

His predecessor, who was only slightly shorter, was being spruced up for the annual Frazee Turkey Festival in July 1998. Just days before the banquet, workers were adjusting the base of the enormous fiberglass bird when it caught fire from the flame of a blowtorch. The entire turkey went up in smoke in a matter of minutes, but not before a passing tourist snapped a couple of Polaroids of the impromptu bonfire.

"Those guys sure got teased after they did that!" says the guide at the tourist bureau. All that remained for the celebration were the charred remains of the gobbler and a new papier-mâché egg, representing a new beginning. The culprits made the best of their blunder by printing T-shirts with a snapshot of the burning bird and the caption, "World's Largest Turkey (Roast)."

"Good thing we already had another one on order!" adds the tour guide. The new turkey was installed a few months later, to accompany the smaller turkey downtown next to a large map of the region. One year later, carnage from the fire was still evident on the ground around Big Tom, in spite of attempts of cover it up with straw. The World's Largest Turkey definitely has reason to be nervous.

World's Largest Turkey. From Highway 10, turn north onto Route 29 and look up the hill to Lions Park.

Frazee's town symbol was getting spruced up for the annual Turkey Fest when it caught fire from a welding torch and went up in flames.

While in the Area

Stop at the little park down Main Street to visit the "Goose Pond Moose," welded of old wood-burning stoves, nails, saw blades, and any other piece of scrap metal that Paul Eppling could find.

For lunch, any restaurant in Frazee will serve the town specialty: roast turkey.

Garrison

Walleye Capital of the World
Happy Fishing Grounds

For once, the Minnesota Legislature was nearly unanimous when it declared the walleye the official state fish in 1965, but some spoilsport—probably stumping for the bullhead—voted "nay" in the 128-to-1 tally. In recognition of the many lunkers hooked in its waters, Mille Lacs Lake was soon after nominated the "Walleye Capital of the World."

On the western shore of this mini-ocean, the residents of Garrison constructed a beautiful portable fiberglass fish (only slightly bigger than those found in the actual lake) to accompany Miss Garrison in the annual town parade. Across the lake, Isle raised a nearly identical fish on Main Street in honor of the tastiest fish in the state.

Garrison's whale of a walleye was no match for a tornado that whipped through town, however, so this fragile fish was affixed to a cement base and now serves as a beacon for boaters and ice fishermen lost on the lake. Signs circle the statue asking tourists to avoid mounting the fish like a jungle gym.

Further north along the Canadian border, however, a sixteen-foot concrete walleye sports a saddle, so tourists can clamber up a ladder to hop on its back. A snapshot of this fish, next to Highway 53 on Lake Kabetogama, shows all your friends back home how truly extraordinary the fishing is in northern Minnesota.

World's Largest Walleye, the shores of Mille Lacs Lake, Garrison. From the Twin Cities, take 169 north to Lake Mille Lacs. Drive about five miles past Grand Casino to Garrison. The fish is on the east side of the road at a wayside rest stop along the lake, just before 169 forks with Highway 18.

No wonder Garrison is the Walleye Capital of the World: it's on the shores of
the best walleye lake in the state.

Grand Rapids

Judy Garland Tour
Follow the Yellow Brick Road

" **I**t's a beautiful, beautiful town," said Judy Garland about her home-town, Grand Rapids. Born in 1922, the heel-tapping wonder started her career at age two, dancing at her father's movie theater in town. Her big debut was at the nearby opera house in Aitkin, and her big break was beating out little Shirley Temple for the lead in *The Wizard of Oz.*

Once Judy hit the big time, she rarely ventured home to Minnesota. In later years, when life took a downturn, she reminisced about her happy, innocent youth in Grand Rapids—the town that will always claim her as its own.

Liberal, Kansas has mysteriously proclaimed itself the home of Dorothy and the "Land of Ahs," complete with what they claim is Dorothy's house from *The Wizard of Oz,* the "true" ruby slippers, and a little museum. Try they might, but Judy Garland herself dubbed Minnesota as "swell," and her real hometown, Grand Rapids, has Judy murals, museums, and festivals that can't be topped.

Judy Jubilee

Grand Rapids immortalizes Ms. Garland every year at the huge Judy Jubilee celebration in June. Lorna Luft, Judy's daughter and Liza Minnelli's half-sister, often stops by to sing a few classics from her mother's twenty-four albums and nearly one hundred singles.

You can "Mingle with the Munchkins," as members of the original Lollipop Guild regularly appear for autographs. Wizard of Oz karaoke breaks out spontaneously, since everyone has been saving up all year to sing "Somewhere Over the Rainbow."

Judy Garland Museum

The Yellow Brick Road in Grand Rapids leads right to the Itasca County Historical Society in the beautiful, one-hundred-year-old Central School. Don't worry about smelling the flowers out front since the poppies have been replaced with begonias. On the second floor is the largest collection of Judy's memorabilia in the country, according to the curators. Although the ruby slippers are replicas, many other original artifacts make it worthwhile.

Old Central School, 10 Northwest Fifth Street, (218) 326-6431. Take either Highway 169 or Highway 2 into the center of town and follow the yellow brick road.

Judy Garland Children's Museum

The huge mural of the happy foursome wandering toward Oz reflects the contents of the building. The original blue gingham dress that

Standing along the Yellow Brick Road like the Emerald City, the Central School houses the largest collection of Judy Garland memorabilia in the world.

Dorothy wore on her trek is on display, along with other *Wizard of Oz* costumes and a sword from the Wicked Witch of the West's castle. Even the old carriage used to carry the characters through Oz is displayed, which just happened to belong to some non–Hollywood type named Abraham Lincoln.

Judy Garland Children's Museum, 19 Northeast Fourth Street (off of Highway 2), (218) 326-1900 or 1-800-664-JUDY. From the south, take Highway 2 toward the center of town and look for the huge mural. Summer only.

Judy Garland's House

"We had a lovely house. . . . We lived in a white house with a garden," recalled Judy Garland. The Gumms lived in their quaint home in Grand Rapids for about seven years (until Judy was four years old) before moving on.

The Gumm house has been moved just past the Sawmill Inn on the ever-expanding edge of town. Poppies spring into bloom along a little yellow brick road leading to the front door. The inside furnishings from 1925 may not be original Gumm, but they set the tone nevertheless. During the Judy Garland Festival, a huge *Wizard of Oz* collectors' and antique show is set up in front of the house.

Judy Garland's House, 2227 Highway 169. From downtown Grand Rapids, go south on 169 and look for the little white house on the right.

Hackensack

Home of Paul Bunyan's Sweetheart
Robert Frost Roadside Attraction

In 1952, grocer Doad Schroeder had a brainstorm: he envisioned an oversized fiberglass woman presiding over scenic Birch Lake in downtown Hackensack. With the first generation of Paul Bunyan statues already old hat, Schroeder worked day and night on Paul's enormous girlfriend. Her hands were placed coyly in front of her, and a curious Trojan horse–like trapdoor was carved into her skirt for repairs.

The town was at a loss for how to baptize Paul's beloved, since campfire stories never revealed much of his private affairs. Even when Robert Frost wrote "Paul's Wife," revealing the gossip behind the giant's love life, he neglected to name the mysterious belle.

Brainerd had ignored Frost's advice that Paul's girlfriend would not be remembered or thought of by name: the town had already chosen the obvious moniker "Pauline" and marched her likeness in lumberjack parades. Schroeder picked the more interesting "Lucette Diana Kensack," and Brainerd and Hackensack have been at odds ever since. To avoid any lawsuits, the Hackensack Chamber of Commerce displays the "official" marriage license, authenticated documents, and other Paul Bunyan memorabilia to prove their case.

The birth of Lucette, however, is more difficult to pin down. Robert Frost's poem gives her an Arthurian Lady-of-the-Lake bent (although she never hands Paul an Excalibur-like ax).

Although the waters of Birch Lake may have given her life, the winds swept across that lake during the winter of 1991 and beheaded poor Lucette as swiftly as a guillotine. Having a decapitated town symbol is murder on morale, so Lucette soon sprouted a new head, thanks to Walker native Jerry Faber. Hackensack stood proud once again.

Next to Paul Bunyan's sweetheart, locals mounted his little offspring, Paul Jr., looking a little stunted next to his hefty mama. Once

Supposedly just Paul Bunyan's "girlfriend," Lucette Diana Kensack shows off her gold ring. Somehow the "platonic relationship" story doesn't hold water—especially with Paul Jr. next to her.

again, Mother Nature was not amused, sending a hailstorm that wreaked havoc on Lucette's fiberglass back, nearly ruining her hands.

Nevertheless, natives come out en masse for the annual Sweetheart Days, celebrating the joyous union in the musical, "The Ballad of Lucette," by the Hackensack Metropolitan Light Opera Company. In spite of these rough times, Lucette peers right down Main Street Hackensack with an air of authority that would make Robert Frost proud.

Lucette Diana Kensack and Paul Jr. statues. Turn west off Highway 371 in downtown Hackensack. Drive past the Up North Cafe and the Yellow Brick Road store; the statues are two blocks from the highway.

Harmony

Crystal Wedding Chapel
Underground Eloping in Niagara Cave

Farmer Kennedy was miffed. Three of his pigs were missing, simply lost without a trace. Not one to believe in alien abduction, he set out searching for the path his pigs had taken. At last he heard a faint "oink" coming from deep within the earth. Remembering that the area around Harmony is known as "Karst Country" for the numerous sinkholes, he scoured the ground until he found the small hole from which the oinks emanated. Farmer Kennedy's son was lowered into the pit with a lantern and found the three pigs in perfect shape, rummaging around in the dark. When the boy shined his torch around, he discovered a beautiful underground waterfall and a whole series of breathtaking caverns.

The porous limestone caves were mapped out, and soon enough, tour groups were led down 150 feet into the earth to see the 60-foot waterfall. "Niagara Cave" rivaled the Wisconsin Dells, House on the Rock, and even Wall Drug for the number of billboards before highway beautification.

A "Crystal Wedding Chapel" was set up and hundreds of marriages have since been consecrated in the chilly, constantly 48° church. Although only a handful of relatives can bear witness to the ceremony, several lovebirds tie the knot underground every year.

The staff at Niagara Cave still spins yarns about the history of the cave and nicknames each stalactite after a recognizable shape or a famous person—like ole Grand Dad Stalactite. The tour ends with screams in pitch-black darkness as the guide switches the lights off in the echo chamber.

Niagara Cave, (507) 886-6606 or 1-800-837-6606. Drive four and a half miles south of Harmony on Highway 139 and follow the signs. Summer only.

Three little pigs fell into a sinkhole and found the most interesting caves in the state.

While in the Area

The nearby Mystery Cave State Park toward Spring Valley stretches ten miles underground. It offers tours of many different lengths, depending on your spelunking expertise. This park boasts fossils dating back 450 million years, when the whole area was covered by ocean.

Mystery Cave State Park, (507) 352-5111 or (507) 937-3251. From Wykoff, the park is four miles south of Highway 16 on Fillmore County Highway 5, then two miles east on County Road 118.

Visitors can't help taking a peek at the horse-drawn farm equipment, basket-making techniques, and Angora goats of the largest Amish community in the state. A few different guided tours are available in Harmony.

If you can't wait for Harmony's famous lutefisk dinner at Greenfield Lutheran Church on odd-numbered years, stop in at Norseland Kitchens on the main street for some lefse and other Norwegian specialties.

Hibbing

Greyhound Bus Origin Center
"From Hibbing to Everywhere!"

The Greyhound Bus Museum is the dream come true for curator Gene Nicolelli. Strangely, when asked if he likes buses, he responds, "Not really. I can hardly tell one from another. I just admire the pioneering spirit!"

Nicolelli was a grocer when he noticed a dusty old sign in the abandoned Hibbing bus depot that read, "Birthplace of the Bus Industry in the United States." Realizing the importance of this little plaque, Nicolelli began researching the forgotten history that put Hibbing on the map.

His quest revealed a disgruntled Swedish immigrant, Carl Erick Wickman, who was sick and tired of mining. Wickman saved what little money he could and bought a Hupmobile agency with one car for sale. Somehow he hadn't considered that no miner could actually afford a fancy horseless carriage. "Everybody wants a ride, but nobody wants to buy a car," he lamented on May 14, 1914. He started charging fifteen cents per test drive, which usually ended up at the rider's job at the Hull-Rust Mine. Frustrated that he couldn't sell the car, Wickman instead started our national bus industry with a two-mile route and his Hupmobile.

This taxi service began making regular trips between Hibbing and Alice in 1914. Together with Andrew G. Anderson, Wickman got out the welding torch and extended the frame of the Hupmobile to fit more seats. Passengers piled on what was probably the world's first bus, but when the engine was fired up, the bus wouldn't budge. The fenders were resting on the wheels, since the suspension couldn't hold so many people. After the miners piled off, Wickman and Anderson hastily attached some leaf springs for shocks, revved up the motor again, and the rest is history. Only later did automobile manufacturers follow their lead and begin producing buses.

Other problems arose for these Iron Range entrepreneurs and their new Mesaba Motors. When the first snowflakes started to fall, they armed their buses with snowplows, clearing the roads long before the state did. One bus was even equipped with tank treads to conquer the biggest snowdrifts. The "first heating system," as shown in the museum, is a mannequin covered with a blanket.

When huge deposits of iron were found under Hibbing, Mesaba Motors chipped in to move the entire town two miles away to Alice between 1918 and 1920.

The Hibbing library saw the initiative taken by Mesaba and set up the world's first bookmobile, bringing books to the hundreds of miners scattered around the Iron Range.

The bus system hooked up with the Great Northern Railroad to extend the passenger lines throughout Minnesota. Finally travelers could

Go with the Hound! From hauling rides on a Hupmobile to moving the masses coast to coast, buses were born on the Iron Range.

buy a ticket directly to their destination. After acquiring several start-up bus lines, the company moved to Chicago, changing its name to "Greyhound" when a comptroller looked at the reflection of a bus in a shop window and noticed that it looked like a race dog. The greyhound became the third most recognized canine in America at the time, after Lassie and Rin Tin Tin.

Having learned all these amazing firsts about his hometown of Hibbing, Nicolelli pleaded with Minnesota governors for fifteen years to get financial backing for a bus museum. He gathered bus collectibles and old drivers donated Greyhound paraphernalia. A little museum was opened in 1989 in Hibbing with original photos of old bus depots, such as the one at First Avenue and Seventh Street in Minneapolis, which became Uncle Sam's and later First Avenue rock club. An interactive bus display puts tourists in the driver's seat to someday win the "Golden Steering Wheel Award" for safe driving.

After years of lobbying, the museum was moved to larger digs in 1999, where actual buses from each era are displayed. Motion detectors set off horns, motors, and tapes telling about the displays. With partial funding from Greyhound and land donated by the city of Hibbing, Nicolelli has realized his dream. "All these Swedes and miners. They didn't know diddly about the bus industry, but look at what they did!" With that entrepreneurial spirit, no wonder their slogan was "From Hibbing to Everywhere!"

Greyhound Bus Origin Center, 1201 East Greyhound Boulevard, (218) 263-6485 or (218) 262-3895. From Highway 169, take the First Avenue exit north into town until the street dead-ends into Howard Street. Take a right, go to Third Avenue and turn left. Go over the railroad tracks and look for the red, white, and blue building on the left. Summer only.

While in the Area

Hibbing is known for Jeno Paulucci and his food empire of Chun King and Jeno's Pizza, but its most well-known offspring is Robert Zimmerman. Born in Duluth in 1941, Robert changed his name to Bob Dillon after his favorite poet, but soon learned the correct spelling and changed it to Bob Dylan. His very first recording, at age three, was sung into a Dictaphone in his father's office in town, and his first band was the Golden Chords, which played in town when he was just a teenager. Dylan's first record earned him just four hundred dollars. But that's okay, since he often shunned success, as when he refused to play on the *Ed Sullivan Show* because he wasn't allowed to play "Talkin' John Birch Society Blues."

If you ask the waitress in the Sportsmen's Café on Howard Street the whereabouts of his house, she will respond, "I don't know where his house is. See, he was a couple years ahead of me in school." At Zimmy's next door, everyone knows and they even have T-shirts for fans.

Bob Dylan's boyhood home, 2425 Seventh Avenue East, blue house (private residence).

After peeping at Dylan's house, stop by the impressive Hibbing High School, which is on the National Register of Historic Places. Just

Robert Zimmerman's childhood home attests to his humble roots. (Bob Dylan's former house is now a private residence.)

imagine the pepfests they must have had in the elegant auditorium with cut-glass chandeliers and murals from the days when money was pouring into town from the mines.

For a snack afterward, stop in the Old Howard on Howard Street for the rustic atmosphere.

Hibbing High School, Eighth Avenue East and Twenty-First Street, (218) 262-3895 or 1-800-444-2246.

Hibbing

World's Largest Open Pit Iron Ore Mine

Near the Town That Moved

The Hull-Rust Mahoning Mine is visible from outer space. This "Grand Canyon of the North" is the product of moving 1.4 billion tons of earth, more than was moved for the Panama Canal.

To make the "World's Largest Open Pit Iron Ore Mine," sacrifices

The ultimate monster truck helped lug millions of tons of ore out of the Hull-Rust Mahoning Mine, creating the "Grand Canyon of the North."

had to be made. Iron deposits were found under the original town of Hibbing, so little by little, buildings were moved. By 1918, the entire town had been shifted two miles away, taking over the little town of Alice. For two years, Hibbing was on the move, and some buildings had to be shifted a few more times over the next forty years as the pit grew.

As the story goes, a man was scheduled to be married at the local church, but the preacher told him, "You'd better get married now, 'cause we're gonna move the church tomorrow." Unfortunately, a lot of these structures weren't built to be mobile homes, and they tumbled into piles of toothpicks.

The remains of part of the old town of Hibbing can still be visited right before the view of the mine. Even the old street signs were left standing in this eerie ghost town.

Hull-Rust Mahoning Mine, (218) 254-3321 or 1-800-372-6437. Take the Howard Street exit off of Highway 169 to Greyhound Boulevard (Third Avenue). Turn right and go north past the Greyhound Bus Museum and the compost dump. Summer only.

Hinckley

Fire Museum

In the Former "Town Built of Wood"

Picking up the phone at the Hinckley Fire Museum is not unlike being a 911 operator. The sound of fire and screaming is heard, then comes a loud voice: "This is a true story of gruesome loss of life, miraculous salvation, and ultimately, a new beginning for both survivors and the earth itself."

"The greatest tragedy in Minnesota history" struck "The Town Built of Wood" due to careless lumbering of the area. The good wood was floating downstream and the ground was left covered with small, dried-out limbs. The arid weather made the entire area a tinderbox ready to explode. Sparks from passing trains probably ignited the fields of kindling, and the inferno swept from town to town.

While the railroad may have caused the fire, engineer James Root and his "rescue train" managed to take some residents to safety as his hands were seared to the burning throttle.

Another hero was Tommy Dunn in the depot agent's office in Hinckley. While residents ran to the gravel pit or the lake to escape the fire, he sent his final message of warning to the next depot in Barnum: "I think I've stayed too long." Fire leaped around him and the building was engulfed in flames.

People could see the smoke all the way into central Wisconsin and Iowa as it burned 320,000 acres and destroyed six towns: Mission Creek, Sandstone, Miller, Partridge, Pokegama, and, of course, Hinckley. In total, 418 people died on September 1, 1894, according to the coroner's official tally.

The mysterious "Wolf Boy" legend sprang from the ashes. A little boy had survived the fire but was so shocked and burned that he went on living in the wilderness near town. Locals reported seeing him foraging through the woods and frequently stopping to drink from the lake. In the dog days of summer, people shivered with fear hearing him howl in mourning.

To bring relief to Hinckley, the depot was rebuilt right away (and is now on the National Register of Historic Places). Once the town was back in working order, a separate waiting room was completed for women so they could be away from tobacco-spitting men, and lodging for the railroad agent was added to this now "first-class" depot.

The building appropriately became the home of the Hinckley Fire Museum, with displays of metal objects melted in the intense heat of the firestorm. Among memorabilia from victims is a huge red mural of the town burning to the ground, reminiscent of Dante's visions of inferno. Until recently, a "Mass Graves" sign pointed tourists to the memorial on the other side of the highway.

Since the fire, Hinckley has changed its motto from "The Town Built of Wood" to "A Place to Stay for More than a Day."

Even though the "Town Built of Wood" burned to the ground, leaving 418 people dead, vast Minnesota forests made wood the preferred material for rebuilding Hinckley and constructing its Fire Museum.

Hinckley Fire Museum, 106 Old Highway 61 South, (320) 384-7338. Take the Hinckley exit off of I-35 west into town, then turn right on County Road 61; the Hinckley Fire Museum is on the left. Summer only.

While in the Area

Tobie's Restaurant has grown by leaps and bounds, but locals prefer the more low-key Cassidy's (I-35 and Highway 48; [320] 384-6129) across the highway. It's a classic Minnesota supper club with a huge salad bar, fresh bread, and famous clam chowder.

Thirty miles north on I-35 is the Fires of 1918 Museum in Moose Lake. After the inferno of 1894, nearly the exact situation happened farther north: dry weather made the conditions ripe for a blaze and sparks from railroad cars probably ignited the fire. As a result of these 1918 fires, 450 people were killed, 52,000 were injured, and damage totaled $73 million. The flames were heading toward Duluth when a last-minute wind shift saved the city but left its neighbor, Cloquet, charred. Logging practices were finally changed to avoid these catastrophes.

International Falls

Grand Mound
Prehistoric Colossus in Frostbite Falls

Where the Rainy and Big Fork Rivers converge, a seemingly normal tree-filled hill rises up. This mound, however, is one of the most mysterious sites in the state.

Guides from the Minnesota Historical Society douse visitors in Repel insect spray to stave off the swarms of mosquitos, then send them on a self-guided tour down the maze of wooden ramps past a series of smaller overgrown mounds to the most ancient construction in the state.

Settlers only realized the importance of this site when they stumbled across four smaller mounds around the base of this huge protrusion. Recognizing the little ones as Indian burial mounds that are common across the state, early surveyors thought that the "Grand Mound" was really something special, even powerful.

None of the Native Americans in the area knew the history of the large burial site, so theories raged about ancient western civilizations setting up shop in northern Minnesota. Could this be Atlantis? Viking Valhalla? A prehistoric extraterrestrial launching pad? Perhaps the Celtic druids built the hill and bestowed mystical powers upon it?

Although certainty in archaeology is never easy, the most likely theory asserts that the ancient Laurel Indians started constructing the mound in about 200 B.C. These woodland people were lured into the area year after year by the ancient giant sturgeon filling the lakes and by the holy cemetery of Grand Mound. Later tribes continued to add to this sacred site for more than a millennium, making it the largest burial mound in the Upper Midwest.

Grand Mounds Interpretive Center, (218) 279-3332. Follow Highway 11 west out of International Falls and look for signs to the Grand Mounds Interpretive Center. Summer only.

Prehistoric Mound, at Mound Park, Laurel Minn.
Height 28 ft. Width 115 ft. One of the largest Mounds found
built by the Prehistoric Race, called "Mound Builders"

In northern Koochiching County, a series of mysterious mounds rises above
the Rainy River, shown here in 1900. The "discovery" of the twenty-eight-
foot-high hills led to wild speculation about their origin.

While in the Area

One of Minnesota's famous roadside landmarks, Smokey the Bear,
stands twenty-six feet tall with two little bear cubs. Gordon Shumaker
of Minneapolis built the beast out of fiberglass in 1954 after years of
specializing in Aquatennial floats. Rangers from nearby Smokey Bear
State Forest diligently checked Shumaker's work so his forest fire vigi-
lante wasn't taller than theirs.

This Smokey the Bear hails from the 1950s and is one of the original roadside sculptures of Minnesota.

Kellogg

Lark Toy Museum

Ticky Tack Tourist Trap

"All I had was seven hundred dollars and a bandsaw," says Donn Kreofsky of his Lark Toy Museum. He called it quits as an art professor at Winona State University and St. Mary's College, then got to work carving hand-painted pull toys for his alternative Toys-R-Us.

His End of the Tale Wood Workshop now puts out more than one hundred thousand toys each year. "I spend most of the day designing. I'll make a sketch, send it down to the woodshop. They'll send it back carved, and I'll decide on what colors to paint it."

While Father Christmas is busy in his workshop twiddling basswood, his wife Sarah will show you around the best toy shop/museum in the state. Different stores under the same roof—like the Ticky Tack Tourist Trap—and displays of classic old games lure shoppers all the way from Germany.

"Here's the choking kids room," Sarah Kreofsky chuckles upon entering the room of collectible old metal toys and lunch boxes, from Betty Boop to Underdog. "The robots live together on this wall," she says, pointing to a huge selection of old-fashioned robots that would make George Lucas green with envy.

Part nostalgia, part thinking games, the toys range from hula hoops and bicycle bells to kaleidoscopes and frog habitats. Even "collectible" Jesse Ventura dolls make an appearance.

Kids can't help but stare at their miniature pot-bellied pig, who's busy grinding his tusks to sharpen them. Everything around "Gip" the pig is spelled backward, "because that's how the elves do it," according to Sarah Kreofsky.

The tour climaxes with the hand-carved carousel, which took Donn Kreofsky ten years to complete. Horses, a giraffe, a swan, and even a dragon take a spin every half hour as kids line up to get on their favorite merry-go-round steed.

Although the Kreofskys originally set out to mass-produce their handmade toys, they opted out of the wholesale business in 1995. "We've been in business for fifteen years; we used to deal with 180 stores nationwide. One day we'd receive an order for nine thousand pull toys for the Smithsonian, then the next we'd get an order for ten thousand from Neiman-Marcus. It got to be too stressful. Now we just do retail through our store and Web Site, so we can meet folks passing through."

Lark Toy Museum, (507) 767-3387. Rather than turning east into Kellogg off of Highway 61, turn west on County Road 18 and follow the signs.

Donn Kreofsky's pet project for ten years was to hand carve this gorgeous carousel as the masterpiece of his Lark Toy Museum. Instead of horses, he carved reindeer, ostriches, roosters, flamingos, and dragons for guests to ride.

Lake City

The Home of Waterskiing

Ralph Samuelson: Daredevil of the Waves

During the summer of 1923, Ralph Samuelson was working on a turkey farm in Mazeppa when he had a vision: he believed he could walk on water. The eighteen-year-old strapped his downhill snow skis on his feet, grabbed a rope behind a speedboat on Lake Pepin, and fell flat on his face. His friends in the boat all had a good laugh.

Ralph swam to shore, and tied a couple of old barrel staves on his feet and went out for another run. After he nearly broke his leg, his amused friends thought it was time to go in for the evening. Ralph begged them to give him another shot. He realized that more surface area under his feet would keep him on top of the waves. A pair of eight-foot boards measuring nine inches wide were secured to his feet with leather straps. He held on to the rope, perhaps gave a thumbs-up, and his buddies gunned the outboard motor. They couldn't believe their eyes. It was fantastic. The boards had snapped in two from the pressure, sending Ralph head over heels into the water. They were awed by his threshold for pain.

That night, Ralph was still determined to realize his dream. He borrowed his mother's wash boiler and curved the tips of a couple boards. He pounded on iron strips to reinforce the wood so he could avoid doing cartwheels for his friends' entertainment. The next morning he met his buddies on the beach with his new invention, and they were only too glad to watch another one of his now famous wipeouts. Ralph clenched the rope with all his might as the boat pulled him to the surface. His friends' jaws dropped as they saw Ralph walking on water.

The entire town came out to see the indestructible Ralph perform his trick skiing. A new bandstand was built along the shores of Lake Pepin to watch this new phenomenon, which even happened behind seaplanes. The rage spread and nearly every lake in Minnesota soon had waterskiers braving the waves.

In time, Ralph's vision became old news around the country, but then a group of Frenchmen had the audacity to claim that waterskiing was invented on the French Riviera. This would not do. After all, it's called *waterskiing*, not *ski nautique!* Lake City loudly protested France's illegitimate claim.

Road signs leading to Lake City now declare it the Home of Waterskiing. Ralph's old skis were rediscovered with a little *RWS* on the tips; they are displayed at the Lake City Chamber of Commerce. A plaque

Not content with walking on water behind a speedboat, Ralph Samuelson, the "Daredevil of the Waves," strapped his line behind seaplanes, showing the crowd gathered at the Lake Pepin bandstand that he could fly (with a little help from huge ski jumps).

was mounted along Lake Pepin where the "Father of Waterskiing" once challenged the waves. Ralph is even quoted as saying, "If I had it to do over again I couldn't have chosen a better place to have it happen than Lake City, Minnesota, on beautiful Lake Pepin."

Lake City Chamber of Commerce, 212 South Washington Street. Turn east off of Highway 61 in downtown Lake City. Go over one block to the Chamber of Commerce to see Ralph Samuelson's skis.

Le Sueur

W. W. Mayo House

Microscope Saves the World

While snake oil salesmen were hawking their wares to gullible invalids, the activities of W. W. Mayo also raised the eyebrows of some wary but thankful patients. Mayo peered through the first microscope in Minnesota, looking at all sorts of cells and other unexplained

This white house in downtown Le Sueur still has the feel of the days when it was built in 1859. W. W. Mayo lived here and began a tradition in medical care that put Minnesota on the map.

phenomena. Although his techniques seemed bizarre and crude at the time, he was the first person in the world to diagnose disease through these high-powered lenses. Today you can tour the quaint Le Sueur house Mayo lived in while he was setting up his shop in Rochester. Guides in period costumes will point out the copy of his microscope, placed on his desk as though the doctor had just been receiving patients.

During the Dakota uprising of 1862, Mayo hurried over to New Ulm to treat war victims. Then, following the mass hanging of Dakota Indians in Mankato, Mayo and other doctors dug up some of the fresh bodies under the cover of night, bringing them home to examine under his famous microscope.

Mayo's reputation grew as he continued his research. Due to the lack of refrigeration in the 1880s, caves were dug into the rock to preserve cadavers for further study.

His son Charles H. Mayo learned alongside his father, and at nine years old was already helping give ether to patients to put them out. The younger Mayo helped establish the world's first blood bank in 1933 and also the first postoperation recovery room. The CT scan is another common practice that was first used at the Mayo Clinic, in 1973.

W. W. Mayo House, 118 North Main Street, (507) 665-3250 or (507) 665-6965. Summer only.

Mayo Clinic, 200 First Street SW in Rochester, (507) 284-2315 or (507) 284-2450.

The last important site of the Mayo tour is the huge Mayowood mansion built in 1911. The fifty-five-room estate overlooks a private lake formed when the Mayos dammed the Zumbro River, which runs through the huge forest. The guestbook is always a favorite place to spot such celebs as Helen Keller, FDR, and the King of Nepal. From humble beginnings and often crude techniques, the name *Mayo* became known and respected around the globe. Mayowood is now part of the Olmstead County Historical Society.

Mayowood, (507) 282-9447. Turn west off Highway 52 on Mayowood Road, then follow the signs to the mansion and grounds on the left side of the road.

Lindstrom

Little Sweden
Välkommen till Lindström

When entering Lindstrom (or is it Lindström?), don't be taken aback if you hear as much Swedish as English. Of course, sometimes it's because groups of Scandinavians visit this little town, which is known even in the old country.

"Ya, it's just like where we come from. They even have Volvos from Göteborg," said a couple from southern Sweden who were visiting the Karl and Kristina Oskar statues in front of the Chisago County Press Office. "Our town Karlshamn in Sweden has the same famous statue of Karl Oskar from Vilhelm Moberg. You know his books *The Emigrants, Unto a Good Land, The Last Letter Home?* They're very good."

At the gas station at the end of town, a defiant Lindstrom local isn't quite so enthusiastic about Oskar. "Oh yeah, he's standing there stone-cold like a Swede," he jokes. The emigrant couple used to march proudly in the annual town festival, but now they're placed next to the emigrant stone, which was sent as a gift from Duvemåla, Sweden.

Scandinavian pride hardly ends there. An enormous blue and yellow mural of the Swedish flag on the side of Cottage Gifts leaves no doubt about its owner's heritage.

Even the writing on the water tower is Swedish. Shaped like a tea kettle with patterns from Scandinavian tole-painting, the water tower proclaims "Välkommen till Lindström." The visiting Swedes yell goodbye in Swedish as I climb into my Volvo and drive away.

Karl and Kristina Oskar statues. Take exit 139 off I-35 east toward Lindstrom. The stoic Swedes will be on the south side of the road in downtown.

Krumkake, lutefisk, lefse, and other Swedish specialties are served in almost any of the down-home cafés in Lindstrom—even the water tower looks like it's brewing fresh Swedish egg coffee.

Under the Swedish flag, Eichten's Cheese-n-Bison deli makes all of its food fresh. To keep the mouse company, an enormous fiberglass bison has been erected along Highway 8.

While in the Area

For a northern European snack, visit the Lindstrom Bakery, which serves up lots of rich baked goods, or stop at the "Break on 8" for their special Swedish almond cake. For more substantial Scandinavian fare, dine at the Swedish Inn, 12960 Lake Boulevard, (651) 257-4072, or the Chisago House in nearby Taylor's Falls, 311 Bench Street, (651) 465-5245.

Heading east on Highway 8 leads right to the big Swedish Village Mall in Center City. Just past it are some enormous mouse and cheese sculptures and a little windmill luring drivers off the road. Eichten's Cheese Shop not only makes its own cheese, but it has a buffalo herd out back. Occasionally the bison manage to hop the fence and wander away, but that's another story. Call (651) 257-1566.

Little Falls

Charles Lindbergh House
The Lone Eagle's Hideaway

In 1927, Charles Lindbergh boarded a single-engine plane in New York and touched down more than thirty-three hours later in Paris a worldwide hero. Having completed the first nonstop solo transatlantic flight, "The Lone Eagle" was given a prize of twenty-five thousand dollars and instant, lifelong fame.

Perhaps to the disappointment of swooning teenagers, Lindy married a woman who was also a pilot and writer, Anne Morrow. Tragedy struck their new family when their son was kidnapped in March 1932 and later found dead. The world was turned upside down by this violent event, and no one quite understood why it had happened. Some speculate that it was a threat to Lindbergh to stay out of politics because of his outspoken views and natural charisma.

Regardless of this suffering, Lindy followed in his father's footsteps. Charles A. Lindbergh Sr. was a U.S. congressman who spoke out against the United States entering World War I, writing a book called *Why Is Your Country at War?* Lindbergh Jr. was also a fervent isolationist—sometimes accused of being a Nazi—and demanded that America stay out of Europe's affairs.

In spite of Lindy's questionable stance on World War II, he won the 1953 Nobel prize for his autobiography, *The Spirit of St. Louis.* In his later years, ecology took over as one of his passions, and he helped set up the Charles A. Lindbergh State Park in honor of his father. Across the street from the park is the family cottage overlooking the Mississippi, which Charles Sr. had built in 1906 as a summer cabin to enjoy during breaks from his congressional duties in Washington. Lindbergh donated the land and the building to the state in 1931.

The Lindbergh House History Center (below the actual home) contains parts of the *Spirit of St. Louis* and his first plane, an old "Jenny" plane from around the First World War. Displays and a short video shed light on this outspoken and mysterious Minnesotan.

Every year in mid-May, dancers from more than thirty countries converge on Little Falls for the Lindy Hop Festival and the anniversary of Lindbergh's transatlantic flight. Reenactments of Lindbergh's feat take place in mid-August.

Lindbergh House History Center, (320) 632-3154. Take Highway 27 west of downtown Little Falls over the Mississippi, turn left on Highway 238 and look for the signs for the Lindbergh House on the left and the Charles A. Lindbergh State Park on the right.

GREETINGS
– from –
LINDBERGH'S
HOME   TOWN
LITTLE FALLS, MINN.

This postcard photograph of the Lone Eagle was taken after his historic transatlantic flight in 1927, which made him one of the most famous men in America.

Madison

Lutefisk Capital, U.S.A.
Lye-Soaked Manna

"**Y**ou've got a parade, we'll come with the codfish," said Dick Jackson of Madison to the *Star Tribune* in 1983 at the dedication of the new town lutefisk statue. "As far as I know, this is the biggest codfish in America."

Although Madison's Lou T. Fisk statue is no longer mobile, it toured other American cities named Madison as a goodwill gesture in 1987. Lou has even paid annual visits to nearby Glenwood—perhaps to challenge that town's claim as the Lutefisk Capital of the World.

After all, Madison boasts the title of the largest amount of lutefisk eaten per capita in Minnesota (and maybe the world). With a population of 1,950, that's a lot of cod. Even the national champion lutefisk eater hails from Madison. Standing nearly seven feet tall, Jerry Osteraas triumphed at the National Lutefisk Eating Contest in Poulsboro, Washington, in 1989, surpassing his personal record of six pounds at one sitting.

If for some reason you don't know exactly what lutefisk is and you dare ask residents of Madison about this unusual passion, the first reaction will probably be utter disbelief followed by pity. Then they'll likely grab your hand and bring you to any supermarket in town to show you the fridges full of the lye-soaked codfish.

One local recipe recommends steaming the lutefisk in the dishwasher to seal in those special flavors. Whatever the secret method for preparing this Scandinavian delicacy, the fish gelatin is inevitably smothered in butter.

This belief in cod extends to the town festivals. Rather than having Crazy Days for the town sidewalk sales, Madison has "Lutefisk Madness." Stinker Days are held at the end of July with a one-mile Uff-Da Walk and a Lou T. Fisk three-mile run. One of the favorite local events is the outhouse race, where contestants carry a biffy with a person inside through a maze.

A huge codfish even adorns the town water tower, and a recent chainsaw sculpture of a lutefisk shows tourists the way to the big cod in the central park. The huge Lou T. Fisk statue cost the town eight thousand dollars in 1983, and locals dress up the fish for special occasions. During Oktoberfest, he becomes a German with special lederhosen; for military parades Lou gets army fatigues; and for the fishing opener he's decked out as a "fisherfish" (even though there are no lakes nearby).

A stop in Madison calls for a praise to cod. "We don't think you can very well ignore a twenty-five-foot codfish," adds Dick Jackson.

Lou T. Fisk, (320) 598-7373. From Highway 75, take the Madison exit; the fish statue is next to the road in J. F. Jacobson Park.

With a vat of lye, Madison's huge cod, Lou T. Fisk, could make enough of the scrumptious fish to cause any Norwegian to drool with anticipation.

Menagha

Saint Urho, Scourge of Grasshoppers
Patron Saint of Finland

Grasshoppers beware of St. Urho! "The patron saint of Finland" chased the grasshoppers out of his country and saved the endangered grape crop. At least that's how the story goes according to Bemidji State University professor Sulo Havumaki, who claims to have been the first to introduce St. Urho to Minnesota. In honor of the ancient holy man, Menagha has erected an enormous statue of the saint, with his pitchfork impaling one of the troublesome insects.

Grapes in Finland? As with many of Minnesota's oversized icons, the legend seems hopelessly exaggerated. As the story goes, ancient Finland was covered with grapes and Finnish wine was known to connoisseurs all over Scandinavia. When the grasshopper plague hit (as it often did in Minnesota—coincidence?), St. Urho saved the day with his enormous pitchfork.

The myth of St. Urho began in the 1950s as a good-natured rebuttal to hordes of Irish drinking green beer and running gaudy floats down streets filled with screaming onlookers. St. Urho's Day falls conveniently on the day before St. Patrick's Day, but the color of the day is purple, not green. The similarity of these "Pied Piper" stories is uncanny, but that doesn't stop the festivities and delicious "grapes-and-grasshoppers" dinners.

In 1975, a contest was announced to develop the true likeness of the mysterious St. Urho. Local Finn Rita Seppala drew the winner, and a woodcarver from Minneapolis was hired to create the original version, but he supposedly took off with the money.

Chainsaw artist Jerry Ward finally finished Menagha's enormous monument to St. Urho in 1982. The publication *A History of St. Urho* shows a picture of the historic raising of the statue on March 19, 1982, with the headline "The Erection of St. Urho."

The twelve-foot-tall oak icon could handle the grasshoppers, but

"Heinasirkka, heinasirkka, menetaalta hiiteen! Grasshopper, grasshopper, go away!" yell the residents of Menagha every year, in honor of St. Urho.

was soon worn down by the elements. The statue has been replicated in fiberglass by the F.A.S.T. company (Fiberglass Animals, Shapes, and Trademarks) of Sparta, Wisconsin. The original wood Urho has been banished to the Menagha cemetery mausoleum.

Finland, Minnesota, claims Urho fever as well, with its twenty-two-foot totem pole of St. Urho on the lookout for grasshoppers. To prove their loyalty, a local musical group, the North Shore Neighbors, even released a 45-rpm single in 1978, "St. Urho's Polka and Finland, U.S.A." On every St. Urho's Day, March 16, the residents of Finland take to the streets for a parade and a Miss Helmi Beauty Pageant.

Menagha wouldn't be left in the lurch without a procession of its own to honor their savior. Chants of "Heinasirkka, heinasirkka, menetaalta hiiteen!" can be heard from every window as residents of Menagha repeat Urho's legendary mantra, "Grasshopper, grasshopper, go away!"

Minnesota was the first state in the union to officially recognize St. Urho's Day in 1975; all fifty states marched in our footsteps and declared St. Urho's Days by the 1980s, although they probably weren't fully aware of the whole story.

St. Urho statue. Take Highway 71 just south of town; the pitchfork-wielding colossus and the Menagha museum are on the east side of the road.

Minneapolis

Bakken Library and Museum

Electric Eels and X Rays Can Cure Anything

As joggers hoof it around Lake Calhoun getting healthy, an unusual medical museum in a renovated Tudor mansion looms over them and could offer a cure or two. The Museum of Electricity in Life chronicles the curative use of electrical current, from animal magnetism to shock therapy. The most important use of electricity showcased in the museum is the wearable pacemaker, first developed in 1958 by Earl Bakken, the founder of Medtronic, which now funds the museum.

A 30,000-volt blast welcomes visitors as a deafening spark is produced from a few turns of the crank on the Wimshurst Electrostatic Generator—or "the big shocky thing," as kids call it.

The oldest uses of medical electricity are exhibited first, such as the primitive shock treatment used by Giovanni Aldini in 1804 to cure a farmhand of melancholy. Electrotherapy was used for everything from relieving gout to curing the common cold, and a trip to the dentist often involved electrified forceps numbing the mouth prior to removing teeth.

Electrical revelations were considered nothing short of godlike at the time, as seen in an ad for a lecture of W. H. Halse from the 1840s:

> Grand Display of Animal Magnetism!
> Discovery of a New World!
> Revelation of the Magnetic World as an intermediate link between
> the Physical and the Spiritual.
> God revealed, as the Triune Magnet of Universal Attraction,
> generative of Peace and Love.

With the "success" of these shocks, women's problems like "hysteria" also received "electric commotions." And to lose weight, women strapped on an electric corset called the Pulvermacher Chain Electric Belt from 1875 and burned pounds away.

Migraines getting you down? Just sit in a pool of water and pull the chain for a blast to the head, and you'll forget all about your pesky headache without hard-to-digest aspirin.

Medical magnetos from 1890s England were harnessed to cure everything from "nervous diseases" and headaches to rheumatism and sore joints. Nikola Tesla inspired the D'Arsonval Spiral, a large cage of high-frequency electromagnetic fields that patients stood inside to cure obesity, gout, diabetes, or whatever else ailed them.

Alexander Graham Bell chipped in, too, with his metal detector, which found a bullet inside President Garfield.

A favorite exhibit in the museum, though not medical, is a strange-sounding electrical instrument invented by Leon Victor Theremin. By moving your hands close to the Theremin, it makes different tones, which have been used in "The Day the Earth Stood Still" and the 1966 Beach Boys hit "Good Vibrations."

Another favorite exhibit is the Electrarium, a mini-aquarium with a wide variety of electrical fish that can be heard as they sense their surroundings, communicate, navigate, or kill their prey through static electricity.

Electric eels were used in ancient Rome to relieve arthritis. In the eighteenth century, invalids used "electric baths" to invigorate the body, placing one foot on the fish and the other in the water for maximum shock.

While some of the cures seem brutal and perhaps simplistic at first glance, they have saved countless lives. Perched on the hill above the lake (no electric eels have escaped yet), the Bakken charts the fascinating history of medical electricity in its museum and 11,000-book library.

Bakken Museum of Electricity in Life, 3537 Zenith Avenue South, (612) 927-6508. Take the Hennepin exit south off of I-94 nine blocks. Turn right on Lagoon Avenue, which merges with Lake Street. Turn left on West Lake Calhoun Parkway, and follow the shore of Lake Calhoun. After about three blocks, you'll see the Bakken Tudor mansion on your right; take a right on Thirty-Sixth Street, then take a right on Zenith Avenue, and you'll be at the entrance to the museum.

Minneapolis

The Band Box

Fasten the Turnbuckles and Serve Up Supper

One of the eternal landmarks along the road remains the diner. These bastions of Americana can be found stuffed between two big buildings, like Al's Breakfast in Dinkytown, or decked out with a chromed dining car interior, like the Ideal Diner in Northeast Minne-

Band Box diners used to be at every major intersection of the city. Somehow this one escaped the wrecking ball and now keeps regulars happy and well fed with its fresh American fries.

apolis. Some drive-ins keep American cuisine alive, too, like the Soda Works Drive-In at Lowry and Marshall in Minneapolis, which brews up its own version of root beer, cream soda, and ginger ale in the summer.

Evoking images of Edward Hopper's all-night café, diners are a dying breed with just a few classics left in the Twin Cities. One of the best is the Band Box.

Butler Manufacturing needed a sideline to its grain silo biz. After working together with Buckminster Fuller on naval housing, it found its calling: diners, prefab little boxes complete with short-order kitchen, bathroom, and space for ten customers, tops. Package up the diner and ship it on a flatbed train, plop it down on a fresh patch of cement, fasten the turnbuckles in the corners to hold the walls up, and ring the dinner bell.

Butler Manufacturing put together fourteen of these little Band Box diners for the Twin Cities, but only the first one remains. This red-and-white Band Box was opened in 1939 by a Jewish couple. The husband, Doc Weisman, changed his name from Harry Wyman to avoid the rampant anti-Semitism of the time. "Minneapolis is the capital of anti-Semitism in the U.S.," wrote journalist Carey McWilliams at the time. "In almost every walk of life, 'an iron curtain' separates Jews from non-Jews in Minneapolis."

The Band Box was open all night and became a magnet for gangsters, with mafiosi running numbers through the diner. When the situation got too hot, the metal blinds would be rolled down until things cooled off.

Isadore "Kid Cann" Blumenfeld—who got his name because he'd be hiding in the can whenever he heard gunshots—used to sit in back and nonchalantly play cards. A gangland killing happened nearby, as Kid Cann allegedly gunned down Walter Liggett, the editor of a Minneapolis weekly, for exposing his bootlegging in 1935. Kid Cann let him bleed to death in an alley off of Nineteenth Street.

Isabel Buri has been eating breakfast at the Band Box almost daily for fourteen years. "When I first came here," she said, "there were lots of different folks." Then she whispers, "There was one that they used to call a 'mobster.'"

New owners Brad Ptacek and Orin Johnson bought the Band Box in 1988, and realized its cultural importance. Isabel has changed her tune now, saying, "The Band Box is important to our neighborhood.

It's so nice to be able to come into a decent place and then . . . then you're here!"

Band Box Diner, corner of East Fourteenth Street and South Tenth Street, (612) 332-0850. From I-94 westbound, take the Eleventh Street exit and turn right. Drive about three blocks (the street turns into Fourteenth Street) and the red-and-white diner will be on the left.

While in the Area

Frank Hall wanted a diner, but couldn't afford one of those fancy pre-fab jobbies. Instead, he shelled out a hundred dollars for a double garage, paid seventy-five dollars to move it, and set up a kitchen and some tables. Since Hall had been a switchman on the railroads, he put his new diner next to the tracks to lure his old coworkers into what was known as "The Hub of Hell."

That was 1950. More than fifty years later, the Diner still serves up supper in the same double garage, with an annex to serve the overflow customers. Since then, Frank's daughter Darlene Hall has taken over the Diner. "They used to call this area 'The Hub of Hell,'" she said. "I call it 'The Hub of Heaven' since there's so many great memories about the area."

"We serve lots of comfort food," she continued, referring to their famous pork tenderloin and hot turkey sandwiches followed by a generous helping of bread pudding or watermelon. The now defunct *Twin Cities' Reader* called it the best greasy spoon in town. Darlene was furious. "I know it's supposed to be a compliment, but we work hard to keep this place clean!"

The Diner, 2545 Twenty-Seventh Avenue South, (612) 729-9821. Take Hiawatha Avenue (Highway 55) south from downtown. Turn left on Twenty-Sixth Street and go one block past the Stardust Lanes.

Al's Breakfast. 413 Fourteenth Avenue SE, (612) 331-9991.
Ideal Diner. 1314 Central Avenue NE, (612) 789-7630.
Soda Works Drive-In. 2519 Marshall Street NE at Lowry, (612) 789-2156.

Smack-dab in the Hub of Hell lies the Diner, set up in an old garage moved from the West Bank in 1950. Follow the neon sign of Frankie's hamburger man to down-home cooking.

Minneapolis

Fort Snelling

Minnesota's First Tourist Destination

A t the junction of the Minnesota and Mississippi Rivers stand the
oldest buildings in the entire state: the Commandant's Quarters
and the Round and Hexagonal Towers of Fort Snelling. Construction
began in 1819 on the castlelike structures, which never saw any fighting, but were often used as a gathering place for local pioneers.

The fort was completed in 1825 and for the next thirty years it was
the meeting point for three different cultures. The white soldiers of the
fort hosted the Ojibwe and the Dakota, who congregated in the fort to
perform dances and Indian sports, as well as to discuss federal policy
and trade at the nearby Columbia and American Fur Companies.

Eastern tourists venturing up the Mississippi spent a couple of
nights at Fort Snelling, loaded up on fresh supplies, and either continued north or hopped back on the riverboat and returned south.

Thousands of volunteers were trained on the grounds for the Union
Army during the Civil War. Fort Snelling became less of a rendezvous
as it processed and trained soldiers for Indian campaigns, the Spanish-
American War, and even World War II.

Although the fort was never threatened militarily, highways were
slated to run right through the old towers in the 1950s. Fortunately,
the state historical society blocked the bulldozers, and the U.S. Department of the Interior designated the fort the state's first National Historic Monument in 1960.

Today, Fort Snelling has been returned to its former glory as a meeting place, with costumed guides leading guests through the grounds.
The year is 1827, so asking "residents" about modern conveniences
generates quizzical looks as they have carefully set aside their digital
watches and cell phones before entering this time capsule.

Old handicrafts are demonstrated, quilts are sewn, and animal hides
are tanned so youngsters can learn about the old days. Fort Snelling

Clothed in an authentic wool uniform, a soldier sweats in the summer sun while guarding the main gate of Fort Snelling.

In 1958, the Minnesota Department of Transportation had big plans to rip down the Old Round Tower, the oldest building in Minnesota, for a freeway. Luckily, the Minnesota Historical Society stepped in and saved Fort Snelling.

was a city unto itself, with a blacksmith, a governing body, and an army store run by the feisty sutler. Go out with a boom as the cannon blasts and the muskets bang when cadets dutifully test their gunpowder during military drills.

Fort Snelling, (612) 726-1171. Take Hiawatha Avenue (Highway 55) south from downtown and look for signs right before Highway 5. Summer only.

Minneapolis

Minnehaha Falls

Lovers' Rendezvous

In the heart of Minneapolis lies a waterfall that has been a congregation spot for Native Americans for centuries. White settlers followed suit, finding that the laughing water and surrounding oak groves made for the perfect picnic park.

Henry Wadsworth Longfellow brought the falls into the international limelight with his 1855 love poem, "The Song of Hiawatha." Although Longfellow never actually visited Minnesota, the story of Hiawatha, the founder of the Iroquois confederacy, and Minnehaha, "laughing water," inspired Minneapolis to name parallel streets, which converge at the falls, after these supposed lovers. A small statue of the sweethearts stands midcreek, just above the waterfall.

Minnehaha park is still a favorite spot for barbecuers, with the added attraction of the restored Minnehaha depot from 1875. Called "The Princess" by conductors because of the showy, gingerbread-style canopy, the depot was one of the busiest stations on the line, carrying hordes of picnickers. No trains pass on the tracks now, but there is talk of Light Rail Transit using the bright orange depot once again.

Winter freezes the falling water into an icicle sculpture. Some brave souls attempt to climb the ice cliff, but park patrols will lock you in the slammer for these daredevil feats.

Canoers and tubers await the high water of spring to wind down Minnehaha Creek from Minnetonka into the heart of the city. Listen for the gushing white water and step out of the boat before jetting over the falls!

Minnehaha Falls and Depot. Take Hiawatha Avenue (Highway 55) south until it meets Minnehaha Parkway. Turn left. Summer only for depot.

A waterfall in the heart of Minneapolis is a nature getaway for city dwellers.
Its laughing waters have inspired poets and lovers for generations.

Two sweethearts carefully tread over the laughing water in Longfellow's legend, "The Song of Hiawatha."

Minneapolis

Foshay Tower
Minnesota's Washington Monument

Amid the blue-glass skyscrapers and parking lots of downtown Minneapolis, a relatively small stone building pokes up in defiance of its oversized neighbors. The Foshay Tower once stood as the tallest building west of Chicago, a tribute to the rise and quick fall of Wilbur B. Foshay.

At the pinnacle of the 1920s stock market, Foshay was making a killing. He spent four million dollars to put Minneapolis on the map with its first skyscraper. Already by 1888, Minneapolitan LeRoy Buffington had received the first U.S. patent for skyscraper construction, and now Foshay applied for two more for his unique design.

The 447-foot-tall Foshay Tower stands as an homage to the Washington Monument obelisk with added art deco details, lavish woodwork, and touches of gold. The grand opening of the skyscraper was the most extravagant bash Minneapolis had ever seen. Foshay hired John Philip Sousa to write a march just for this occasion, which the composer personally conducted for all the VIPs.

Just two months after the inauguration of his dream, the stock market crashed and Foshay was broke. Sousa's check bounced for "The Foshay Tower Washington Memorial" because he had delayed cashing it. To make matters worse for the penniless Foshay, indictments on counts of mail fraud caused him to be locked up in Leavenworth Prison. FDR came to his rescue in 1935, offering him a pardon.

Foshay's extravagance has survived the notorious Minneapolis wrecking ball and its peak still pokes through the skyline as the sixteenth-tallest skyscraper in the city. Tourists can peer out from the observation deck and imagine when this was the tallest tower west of the Mississippi.

Foshay Tower, 821 Marquette Avenue, (612) 341-2522. From I-94 westbound, take the Eleventh Street exit to Marquette Avenue and turn right.

Imagine John Philip Sousa strutting his band in front of Minneapolis's first skyscraper with a march written just for the occasion. But Wilbur Foshay couldn't pay the bills for his fabulous bash after Black Thursday drove him into the poorhouse (and the jailhouse).

Minneapolis

Lake Harriet Trolley and Museum

The Mob and GM Dismantle the Streetcars

Horses pulled the first public transportation through the Twin Cities on iron tracks, but they were even dirtier than future smog would be. "Each horse would excrete 15 to 30 pounds of manure each day, a lot of which was not removed from the city streets," according to North St. Paul city records.

By 1889, electric trolleys zipped through the streets as terrified pedestrians leaped out of the way of sparks from the tracks and over-head lines. Passengers nauseous from the bumps chomped on gum to hold their lunches down and complained of the winter cold in the windowless carriages. Nevertheless, ridership skyrocketed. Thomas Lowry, "The Streetcar Man," constantly laid new track from Anoka to Hastings and from Stillwater to Minnetonka, mostly to increase the value of his newly developed real estate.

While this extensive web of lines has been mostly ripped up, the Minnesota Transportation Museum has revived one of the most popular lines, from Lake Harriet to Lake Calhoun. Beautifully restored, the antique streetcars run every evening in the summer for a trip back in time to when 523 miles of track crisscrossed the city.

A replica of the old depot has been built, housing a mini–trolley museum with models of double-decker streetcars, photos of tram-filled Minneapolis, and old ticket stubs for day trips to White Bear Lake, Fort Snelling, and Como Park Zoo.

Passengers inevitably ask the conductors why the streetcars disappeared when nearly everyone has fond memories of them. The first threat to trolleys came from posh bicycling clubs around the turn of the century, who insisted the city council spruce up the downtown dirt roads for smoother pedaling. Cyclists were fed up with catching tires in trolley tracks and being run off the road by clanging trams. Debate raged about whether to pave dirt roads with macadam, wood from endless northern forests, or steel from the Iron Range.

The real menace came from General Motors, Standard Oil of California, Phillips Petroleum, Mack Trucks, and Firestone Tires, who teamed up behind the National City Lines (NCL) bus company to dismantle American cities' streetcars. NCL president Roy Fitzgerald hailed from Eveleth, Minnesota, where he had founded the Range Rapid Transit Company. Although he humbly described himself as "one of five farm boys trying to run a few buses," he led the battle to convert eighty cities from streetcars to buses by 1946. The trolleys were often burned and the tracks ripped up, so reverting back to streetcars would be impossible. GM knew that public money, specifically the gas tax, would go toward improving roads and increasing U.S. citizens' reliance on the automobile.

Within twenty-seven months, all the streetcars disappeared from the Twin Cities. Some of the newer streetcars were sold off to Newark, Cleveland, and Mexico City (where they are supposedly still running).

Three of the trams have been restored and now run on the Harriet-Calhoun line. According to the trolley museum, the Minneapolis City Council has tentatively approved extending the line almost into Uptown

This postcard (postmarked 1916) features a scene of Lake Harriet streetcars that are still visible today. Of the one thousand streetcars that criss-crossed the city, three have been restored and putter down a mile section of the Como-Harriet line, rebuilt in 1970.

and opening another line along Minnehaha Parkway to connect to the scheduled Light Rail Transit (LRT) lines.

Lake Harriet Trolley and Museum, (612) 228-0263 or 1-800-711-2591. From I-94, take the Hennepin exit south sixteen blocks. Turn right on Thirty-Sixth Avenue, then left around Lake Calhoun. Turn left at the first stoplight, then right at Lake Harriet until the Linden Hills Depot is in sight. Summer only.

Minneapolis

Museum of Questionable Medical Devices

From Radium Massages to Electroshock Therapy

Deep in a dungeon along the banks of the upper Mississippi lies an array of torture devices that were once thought to cure everything from the common cold to unenthusiastic "pelvic organs." Many of the gadgets came from before the creation of the U.S. Food and Drug Administration, which began regulating drugs in 1906 and medical devices in 1938.

The jolly curator, Bob McCoy, began his collection when a friend gave him a bizarre Psychograph Phrenology Machine from 1905 that deduces all thirty-two personality traits and mental faculties—including "sexamity," "suavity," and "sublimity"—simply by reading the bumps on your head. He was so taken with the devilish device that whenever he saw old "medical marvels," he quickly snatched them up. To attract tourists, the St. Anthony Main shopping district donated a storefront, as long as no admission was charged. The collection blossomed with dangerous "curative" contraptions culled from the American Medical Association and the Bakken Library in Minneapolis.

McCoy has featured the most bizarre mechanisms from his "Quackery Hall of Fame" on *The Late Show with David Letterman* and *The Tonight Show with Jay Leno,* and once gave a fake lecture to an awestruck University of Minnesota medical class demonstrating how his Toftness Radiation Detector could extract "noxious energy from the body."

Thanks to the Museum of Quackery's mix of the absurd and the educational, the *New York Times* dubbed the site one of the five best tourist locations in the Twin Cities in 1998.

McCoy will happily treat the most gullible hypochondriacs. Drop your drawers, doff your top, stare into the 1000-watt lightbulb of the Specto-Chrome, and let the radiation sink into your pores. If the little lights that go "ping" flash red, it's your heart; purple, the evil cancer;

green, too many White Castles; and yellow, your mind is kaput. If that doesn't tell us enough, perhaps putting a blood, urine, or saliva sample under the Omnipotent Oscilloclast from the 1920s can diagnose your "vibration rate." Your Rx? Drink a glass of water that has been blasted with your particular vibration rate from a line of radio tubes.

Let's say your unmentionables aren't behaving, then it's time to activate your "abdominal brain." With the miraculous G-H-R Electric Thermitis Dilator footlong rectal probe and prostate gland warmer from 1918, your nether regions can be warmed to a toasty 100°. Combined with a special ultraviolet comb complete with anal and penile accessories, your sex life will never be the same again.

Too extreme? How about a nice delicate Magik Radium Massage: "When massaged into the sex parts acts as a healthy tonic and stimulant, especially to the testes . . . the parts begin to take on a more healthy glow and appearance, and shrunken tissues begin to fill out and become plump." Or maybe some radioactive Vita Radium Suppositories from 1926 to help "restore failing manly vigor and overcome apathy in women."

To be a manly man, turn to:

> The Vital Power Vacuum Massager [which] Invigorates, Enlarges Shrunken and Undeveloped Organs. It is impossible for a woman to love a man who is sexually weak. To enjoy life and be loved by women you must be a man. A man who is sexually weak is unfit to marry. Weak men hate themselves. Upon the strength of the sexual organ depends sexual strength, in both men and women, furnishing the ambition and energy for all advancement in life. It is a well-established scientific fact that musicians, financiers and pugilists are men of exceptionally strong sexual power.

Medicine for dieting has always been a cash cow for pharmaceutical companies. In the old days, if you were getting a little broad in the beam, you could just pop some special pills with tapeworm eggs for instant weight loss, no matter how much you ate.

Another famous cure-all in the museum is the White Cross Electric Vibrator chair, which "Cures these diseases: Rheumatism, Headache . . . Constipation . . . Lumbago, Catarrh, Scalp Diseases," and so forth. After all, "VIBRATION IS LIFE!" Nowadays, the idea of this device has simply been changed to "magic fingers" for an especially erotic night in bed.

If none of these cures has helped, you might as well give up, since

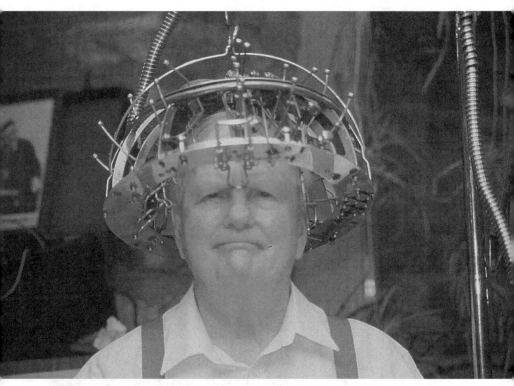

"You ought to have your head examined!" exclaim ads for the Psychograph machine from the 1930s. Curator Bob McCoy graciously displays how his entire personality can be revealed by the bumps on his head, thanks to the scary screws, wires, and bolts of his phrenology machine.

you must have "Poisoned Blood," as an ad for Hot Springs, Arkansas, claims. This bad blood "leads to dismal thoughts and frequently to suicide. . . . Nothing to look forward to but a life of misery and loneliness." When a miracle cure for poisoned blood is found, you can be sure the Museum of Questionable Medical Devices will have the remedy.

Actual Size
of Vita Radium
Suppositories

Museum of Questionable Medical Devices, 219 Southeast Main Street, (612) 379-4046. Take Hennepin Avenue north through downtown. After going over the Hennepin Avenue bridge, turn right onto Main Street. The museum is in the basement of St. Anthony Main.

While in the Area

Slip on your dancing shoes on and waltz over to Nye's Polonaise, 112 East Hennepin Avenue, (612) 379-2021, for some two-stepping to the World's Most Dangerous Polka Band. Then for a little schmoozin' and croonin', peer in the piano bar and belt out your favorite show tunes while Lou tickles the ivories.

Minneapolis

Ray Crump's Baseball Hall of Fame
Build It and They Will Come

Ray Crump began his career when he was thirteen years old, as a batboy for the Washington Senators. He was in Washington the day Mickey Mantle pounded the ball over the fence for the longest homerun ever, 562 feet. He was around when Fidel Castro tried out for Calvin Griffith but didn't make the cut. Castro also pitched a couple of innings for the Havana Sugar Kings against the Minneapolis Millers in 1960. Disappointed with his dead-end pitching career, Castro went home to Cuba and staged a revolution. Crump, on the other hand, started a museum.

Crump became the Senators' equipment manager and moved with them when they became the Twins in the 1960s. "I didn't even know where Minneapolis/St. Paul were. I only knew where International Falls was since it's so cold—'The Icebox of the Nation.' Sports put the Twin Cities on the map!" he says.

Crump lists the events he witnessed: he saw Tony Oliva become the American League Rookie of the Year in 1964; he attended the All-Star Game at the Met in 1965 with Hank Aaron and Willie Mays; and he watched Harmon Killebrew smack 573 homeruns. Crump can also show photos of celebrities, from Leif Garrett to Bob Hope, who hobnobbed with him at the Carleton Celebrity Room.

He has graciously let the world in to see his personal memorabilia at "Ray Crump's Original Baseball Hall of Fame of Minnesota." Even non–sports fans are amused by his "Wall of Celebrities," with photos of himself backstage with the Beatles and an Elvis Corner of Crump and the King.

Crump is no stranger to fame himself, since he's appeared on television 111 times, with countless articles written on his museum. Apart from appearances in *Sports Illustrated* and on *Good Morning America,* he's found time to put his life in words in *Beneath the Grandstands,* his autobiography.

You may not know who Ray Crump is, but a lot of celebrities do: not only is his Minnesota Baseball Hall of Fame full of sports figures and paraphernalia, but a corner of the museum is dedicated to his meeting with Elvis and an entire wall is devoted to photos of him with everyone from Clancy the Cop to Leif Garrett.

All this publicity attracted 111,000 people to his little museum in one year, a number many art museums would covet. After all, where else can you walk on artificial turf from the Metrodome, admire 10,260 signed baseballs, see the first uniform Kirby Puckett ever wore, and look at Harmon Killebrew's last uniform?

If this is too much, take a rest in a chair made of old baseball bats, and watch a video on how to make a Louisville Slugger bat. Or slouch into one of the old bleachers from Met Stadium. Of the stadium controversy, Crump says, "If the Twins moved to St. Paul, I'd stay right here."

It would seem that Crump would have a hard time tearing himself away from ball games across the street to run his museum and gift shop, but he claims,"I haven't been over there to sit down at a Twins game since I stopped working for Carl Pohlad in 1984." He adds that "Carl Pohlad has never set foot in here. He's only dropped people off and waited outside for them while listening to the speakers."

Crump points to an impressive framed collection of baseball cards, including a photo of Calvin Griffith that was a gift from Pohlad to Griffith. "The day after Pohlad bought the Twins," Crump says. "Calvin Griffith called me up and said, 'Ray, come over and get this damn thing out of my house right now!'" Crump was there within the hour to add yet another collectible to his museum.

Ray Crump's Baseball Hall of Fame, 910 South Third Street, (612) 375-9707. From I-94, take the Fifth Street exit west toward the Hubert H. Humphrey Metrodome. Circle the dome, and the museum is across the street on the northeast side.

Minneapolis

Minneapolis Sculpture Garden and Loring Park

Cherry Spoon and Glass Fish

A huge spoon with a cherry squirting water has become the unofficial symbol of Minneapolis. Any tour of the town must pass Claes Oldenburg and Coosje van Bruggen's Spoonbridge and Cherry for a photo op with the skyline jutting up in the background. The public art extends from the Ole Bull statue in Loring Park over the Irene Hixon Whitney Bridge (designed by Siah Armajani) to the Minneapolis Sculpture Garden, where huge hedges separate courtyards filled with abstract sculptures, ready to be explored and enjoyed by children and adults alike.

The Minneapolis Sculpture Garden is the largest urban sculpture park in the world and has been a boon to attendance at the Walker Art Center, even if the garden's lack of Minnesota sculptures is always a sore spot to local artists. Could the world-famous modern art museum be worried that a five-story Jolly Green Giant peering into downtown would dwarf their statues, becoming the highlight of their collection?

The perfect cure for cabin fever in subzero temps is a walk into the Sculpture Garden's greenhouse to sniff blooming flowers and admire the glass fish above the fountain constructed by Frank Gehry, who later designed the stainless steel Weisman Art Museum.

After strolling through the garden (open year round), venture into the actual Walker Art Museum, or put on your tuxedo or mink and catch a show next door at the Guthrie Theater. With a little luck, maybe the notorious Guthrie ghost will rattle its chains!

The walking tour continues over the blue and yellow bridge into Loring Park. In winter, skaters risk the thin ice on the pond, and for six weeks starting each July, the Walker stages bands and films in the park on Monday evenings, while spectators picnic and swat mosquitos.

Lunalux Studio, overlooking Loring Park, is a fascinating blast to the past with old style letterpress machines from the turn of the century. In this age of computers and the Internet, Lunalux preserves the written word with classy offset printing, stationery, and fountain pens.

For lunch, Ruby's Diner next door serves up fantastic southern breakfasts complete with hominy grits. On the other side of Lunalux lies the Loring Café and Bar, about which out-of-town visitors inevitably comment, "It's just like New York!" Regardless, the food is fantastic (but expensive) and the atmosphere is an unusual theater set with gold painted trim, plush red velvet chaise lounges, and a view of Loring Park.

Walker Art Center and Sculpture Garden, 725 Vineland Place, (612) 374-3701. From eastbound I-94, take the Hennepin exit and follow it south. The Walker Art Center is at the junction of Hennepin and Vineland on the west side of the road.

Lunalux Studio, 1618 Harmon Place, (612) 373-0526.

The showpiece of the largest urban sculpture garden in the world, Claes Oldenburg and Coosje van Bruggen's Spoonbridge and Cherry (or is it Paul Bunyan's Spoon?) has become a symbol of Minneapolis. A local band even named one of its records "Under the Cherry Spoon."

Minneapolis

Weisman Art Museum
Not Another Brick Lump

The strangest building in Minnesota began with a fish story. With a lake around every corner, huge statues of trout, northerns, and walleye dot the landscape. To show "the one that got away," braggarts inevitably stop by these fiberglass giants to pose for postcard-style photos.

The fish in this story wasn't built of fiberglass, but instead with hundreds of glass shards glued on top of each other to create the scales; this fish reigns twenty feet over a glassed-in fountain. The internationally recognized and award-winning architect Frank O. Gehry envisioned this towering beast for the Minneapolis Sculpture Garden, the largest urban sculpture park in the world. The Walker Art Museum had purchased the sculpture as part of an exhibit of Gehry's works in 1986, which brought him "a national audience," according to the *New York Times*.

This love affair between Gehry and Minneapolis had begun even earlier, with the unusual Winton Guest House he built in Wayzata in 1983. After the success of this house, the "Standing Glass Fish Sculpture," and the exhibit at the Walker, the University of Minnesota commissioned him to build a museum to house their art collection. Perhaps the embarrassing theft of an Andy Warhol print in broad daylight from one of the stairwells of the university library led to the creation of a stainless steel fortress that could foil crooks' schemes.

Usually architects begin their design with a box, then add other boxes as necessary. According to Gehry, "They told me not to build another brick lump." His original sketch for the building is projected on one of the interior walls of the museum and looks just like a three-year-old's scribble. "It's at this point that the client gets nervous," he pointed out in a speech in Italy.

Only upon seeing the completed museum does one really appreciate Gehry's genius. Curved stainless steel skirts flow in every direction without a parallel line in the bunch. Purple and red rays shoot out in every direction as the buffed surface serves as a giant mirror for the setting sun and the river below.

When the Weisman Art Museum was completed in 1993, reviews were mixed at best. Since then, Frank Gehry has become one of the premier architects in the world, with such works as the American Center in Paris, the Fred and Ginger building in Prague, and the Guggenheim Museum in Bilbao, Spain (a larger version of the Weisman, which has now been called "Baby Bilbao"). Perhaps this international recognition

The Weisman Art Museum became the new look for the University of Minnesota in 1993. Thirteen million dollars of private donations and a comprehensive and stunning art collection have made this bizarre stainless steel structure a mecca for art aficionados.

will help Minnesota truly appreciate the strangest—and possibly most beautiful—building in Minneapolis.

Weisman Art Museum, 333 East River Road, (612) 625-9683. From northbound I-35W, take the University of Minnesota exit; keep right, taking the East Bank exit. Follow the exit ramp, crossing over the Washington Avenue bridge; take the first right to River Road and the museum garage entrance.

Before the Weisman Art Museum, Frank O. Gehry's first splash in the Twin Cities came in the form of a fish. Floundering above a fountain, the see-through statue is the centerpiece of the Cowles Conservatory of the Minneapolis Sculpture Garden.

Mora

World's Largest Dala Horse
Swedish Craft, American Style

The winter of 1716 was a bitter one in Scandinavia. King Charles XII of Sweden was marauding across Europe while his troops at home were forced to seek shelter among civilians. In the Dalarna province, one of these soldiers staying near Mora carved a little horse and painted it an orange-red—a common color in the area because of the copper mine at Falun. He gave the statuette to the little boy of his host family in appreciation for their hospitality.

Other soldiers saw how a gift horse got them a bowl of soup. The carvings became almost a de facto currency and are credited with helping the Swedish army survive the brutal winter. Soldiers even whittled and painted rooster and pig figurines, but the symbol of Sweden became the popular Dala (Dalecarlian) Horse.

A few life-sized versions of the horse exist around Sweden, but the Jaycees in Mora, Minnesota, wanted a giant version of the statue. The plaque at the base of the enormous orange horse hails it as "a reminder of their cultural heritage" and perhaps more importantly as "a tourist attraction."

Hundreds of cross-country skiers swish into Mora for the Vasaloppet, the second largest cross-country ski race in the country; they can't help but pay homage to the more than twenty-two-foot-high horse. In the summer, a water park opens next door, in the shadow of the orange and red beast, which is almost close enough to be used as a high dive.

With Swedish and American flags flying at the same level as the horse's head, the equine stands as a symbol of the sister city of Mora, Sweden. According to the polite town brochure, "nowhere in North America—does there exist a Dala Horse as large as the one that stands at the southern edge of Mora." Other town pamphlets are less cordial to the Swedish Mora, calling it simply the World's Largest Dala Horse.

Dalecarlian Horse. The huge orange horse is just south of downtown Mora on Highway 65.

While in the Area

De Dutch Huis in town has good ethnic food, but Wild Things Pizzeria (30 Union Street North, [320] 679-3346) in downtown Mora has the most unusual atmosphere. While you munch on the Meat Eater's Supreme Pizza, you can't help but feel your place at the top of the animal kingdom with all the stuffed game in the room. Critters from around the world make up the decoration: an African goat, a Dall sheep from Alaska, walleye (of course), a pheasant, a pine martin, a raccoon, a wild boar (from Tennessee?), a Canada goose, a coyote, a lion, a redhead duck, a red deer, and so forth. Apparently, no irony is intended for the "Game Room" sign to the back room.

Weighing a hefty three thousand pounds, this Swedish-style horse stands more than twenty-two feet tall. Finished in 1971, the World's Largest Dala Horse was erected as part of a sister city project with Mora, Sweden.

Nevis

World's Largest Tiger Muskie
Into the Mouth of the Beast

With a boat for one in every six Minnesota residents, fishing is not something to be taken lightly. Early tourism ads for Minnesota called it the "happy hunting and fishing grounds," and even now we are first in the country for per capita sales of fishing licenses.

Because of this obsession with fishing, various towns around the state have boldly declared themselves the hottest fishing holes in the land. Many have erected icons to this pastime, hoping to spread the good word to passing tourists. Bemidji, Bena, Cambridge, Clarks Grove, Deer River, Finland, Garrison, Isle, Madison, Medina, Minneiska, Nevis, Orr, Park Rapids, Rockville, and Rush City all have big fish statues, mostly walleyes.

Nevis, however, raised its monument to the "great white shark" of Minnesota lakes: the tiger muskie. Stories of children losing limbs to hungry muskies have become northwoods legends, and anytime a hungry sunfish nips at a swimmer, tales surface of the muskie that got away.

Governor Luther Youngdahl inaugurated the World's Largest Muskie in 1950, with plenty of jokes about fishing and Swedes. Over the years, however, the thirty-foot-long homage to the muskie, built with ribs of wood and scales of cement, began decaying due to rough winters. Then in 1990, a real fifty-four-pound muskie was hauled in on a Minnesota lake, breaking all previous records and spurring renewed interest in this landmark. A fresh coat of paint and a new roof now keep the fish fresh, so everyone coming to Muskie Days in July can marvel at the muskie (and of course pose in its mouth).

World's Largest Tiger Muskie, downtown Nevis. Take Highway 34 from Walker fifteen miles west. Nevis is on the north side of the road and the muskie statue is in the town park, which you come to as you enter town.

Recently restored, the vicious tiger muskie of Nevis doubles as a jungle gym for picnickers in the town park.

New Ulm

Little Deutschland

Lederhosen, Schnitzel, and Beer

Visiting the Minnesota River Valley town of New Ulm is a trip back into the Old World. Most stores have Teutonic names, like Guten Dag Haus, Heidelberg, Glockenspiel Haus, and Domeier's German Store. Locally born legend Whoopee John probably haunted Brown's Music to pick up an extra accordion for the next Oktoberfest.

For the best lederhosen viewing, this German haven must be toured when the polka bands are playing: during Oktoberfest, Heritagefest in mid-July, or Fasching, on the weekend before Ash Wednesday. If you're lucky, the Heinzelmännchen gnome family will be wandering around with their oversized hats, or perhaps you'll catch the annual Tuba Mania concert, with hundreds of the brass instruments booming through the streets. In any case, accordions, bratwurst, and beer will be around every corner.

Schell's Brewery

First stop is the beautiful Schell's Brewery and Garden on the edge of town. Wander with the peacocks through the maze of flowers and shrubs in front of the old stone mansion, then stop in the beer museum to peruse the old brewing equipment and advertisements. Schell's beer must be good if an ex–all-star wrestler like Baron Von Raschke, a "Brewmeister wannabe," plugs it in their ads.

Old World Brewery tours meander through the enormous copper kettles and boiler rooms, then end in the ever-popular tasting room, where visitors can sip the different brews. During prohibition, Schell's made nonalcoholic "near beer" and root beer, now revived as "1919." During those years, a secret still was set up out in the woods to produce bathtub gin to mix with the near beer.

"Have any of you ever tasted 'moonshine'?" asks the tour guide. "First it takes your breath away, your hair stands on end, and your legs

go numb. If you survive all that, you go deaf in one ear! It's much better to just drink Schell's."

Schell's Brewery, Mansion, and Park, Twentieth South Street and
Payne Street, (507) 354-5528. From downtown New Ulm, go southeast
of town on Highway 68 (Broadway Street). Turn right on Sixteenth
Street and follow the signs.

Hermann the German

Hoisting all those beer steins can make anyone's arm tired, so it's time
to shake a leg with a hike to Hermann's Heights to visit Hermann the
German. Three flights of steps up give a breathtaking view of the
city—no wonder locals flock to the park to roast bratwurst and
knockwurst.

Hermann the Cheruscan was immortalized with this huge copper
statue in 1897, standing as one of the tallest statues in the state. Measuring 32 feet high, Hermann projects a whopping 102 feet in the air with
his base, a constant reminder to residents of New Ulm of their heritage.

Although Gwyn Headley, in her book *Architectural Follies,* dis-
respectfully dubs the statue a "hideous temple monument" and "ir-
redeemably ugly," the author was clearly oblivious to the fact that
Hermann united Germany and kept the Romans on their side of the
Rhine in 9 A.D. No small feat.

Hermann the German, (507) 359-8344. From downtown New Ulm,
turn southwest off Broadway Street (Highway 68) away from the river
on Center Street. Go up the hill and look for Hermann standing tall.

Glockenspiel

The Glockenspiel chimes at noon, 3:00 P.M., and 5:00 P.M., with all the
town characters dancing in circles, giving a ten-minute history lesson
of the town from pioneers to Indian battles to polka two-steppers.
Thirty-seven Dutch bells play the tune for the hand-carved Native
American, bricklayer, brewer, oompah-pah band, and, of course, dancing Germans in lederhosen.

In 1980, thirty-one states and fifty-one Minnesota cities donated
money to build the first freestanding carillon clock tower in North
America. Critics complain the forty-five-foot tower seems cold and
modern, but they usually change their tune when the clock chimes and
the figurines twist to the tunes.

Just as Hermann fought to free the Fatherland of roaming Romans two millennia ago, he now keeps picnickers company as they munch on knockwurst in New Ulm. A Cheruscan warrior, Arminius (or simply Hermann) serves as the town lightning rod, standing thirty-two feet high on top of a seventy-foot cupola.

The leitmotiv hammered out on the thirty-seven carillon bells lays down the rhythm for the frolicking frauleins, the beer stein–tipping merrymakers, and the Dakota, all spinning in harmony. The Glockenspiel's utopian town microcosm dances every day at noon, 3:00 P.M., and 5:00 P.M.

Glockenspiel, Schonlau Plaza at Fourth North Street and Minnesota Street.

Wanda Gág House

Just up the street from the Glockenspiel lies the home of New Ulm's most famous daughter, illustrator Wanda Gág. She grew up in this charming Victorian house, which is now a museum, then later in her life she moved to the East Coast, where she wrote her most famous children's book, *Millions of Cats,* and other stories, and established herself as a well-known artist. A permanent collection of her work is on display at the red-and-white Brown County Historical Museum at Broadway and Center Streets. One of her most famous paintings, of the Dakota Massacre of 1862, is in the rotunda of the Minnesota State Capitol in St. Paul.

Wanda Gág House, 226 Washington Street at the corner of Third North Street.

Suppertime

New Ulm doesn't lack for hearty helpings. Veigel's Kaiserhoff (221 North Minnesota Street, [507] 359-2071) is one of the favorites, where even the "Don Brunner Weight Watcher Special" contains one-third of a pound of hamburger.

Pigs can fly at the Kaiserhoff, where winged pigs hang overhead to get guests in the mood for their impressive schnitzel, sauerkraut, and hot German potato salad. Their knack for cooking pork was even honored by the Pork Producers Association, as shown in a framed article.

Try out the Lewie Bensen Special, which doesn't mess around with diet programs and heaps on the tasty BBQ ribs. The rich flavor of everything on the menu prompted one diner to ask if the breadsticks are fried. "Yes ma'am," the waitress replied, "otherwise they wouldn't taste so good." Schell's robust beer rounds out the meal.

If the Kaiserhoff is full, check out Lamplighter's Bar across the street for robust American food and a wide variety of Schell's beers.

"The Way of the Cross"

After all this merry-making, it's time to repent for your sins. Behind the New Ulm Medical Center, up the opposite hill from Hermann, is the sobering "Way of the Cross," created for Our Sorrowful Mother.

The way was built in 1904 by sisters of The Poor Hand Maids of

Wanda Gág's childhood home has been beautifully restored and is now open to the public as a museum for fans to peruse the work and inspirations of this artist and writer.

Jesus Christ in honor of the "Agony of Our Lord in the Garden of Gethsemane." These nuns heaved wheelbarrows full of cobblestones up Loretto hill to assemble fourteen stations of the cross, including "Agony in the Garden," "Jesus is Condemned to Death," "Jesus takes the Cross on his shoulders," "Jesus falls the 1st time under the Cross," and "Jesus meets his grieving mother."

Each somber statue was imported from Bavaria, and according to the entrance sign, they show the "postures and facial expressions that carry the message of Christ's suffering."

The Way of the Cross, 1324 Fifth South Street. From Broadway Street (Highway 68), turn southwest, away from the river, on Fifth Street. The park is just past the hospital on the right.

New York Mills

Art Park and Philosophy Parade
Home of the Great American Think-Off

A monument to farming has been raised along Highway 10. A huge silhouette of a tractor, with wheels twelve feet tall, stands as a landmark to what has made Minnesota strong. Ken Nyberg of Vining was commissioned to weld this colossus, which has become the symbol of New York Mills, where its likeness is displayed on banners hanging from the town light poles.

Upon closer inspection, you see that a whole series of sculptures rings the tractor. Geese are welded together out of old watering buckets, and dinosaurs evolve from dried cow skulls, deer antlers, and lawnmower blades. In keeping with Nyberg's towering masterpiece, metal corn sculptures mimic the surrounding fields.

This penchant for the cerebral doesn't stop there. Every year, New York Mills hosts a philosophy parade in mid-June, climaxing with the Great American Think-Off. A topic is chosen that has stumped eggheads since Aristotle. Does God exist? Is there a meaning of life? A heated public debate by the final four thinkers ends with the audience settling the contest and choosing the most enlightened debater.

The headquarters of this creative energy is the cultural center on main street. Workers from the enormous Lund Boat factory, which put the town on the map, can walk a block over to this artistic oasis to see concerts and art exhibits, or to participate in art classes.

Next door at the local 3.2 watering hole, the bartender is cooking up burgers on a little hotplate for a couple customers as the pinball machines buzz in the back. The bar is dark but homey. When asked about all the artistic ventures in town, the farmers at the bar don't say much. They're interested, but it's not their cup of tea. Then one of them sounds a note of approval, "But that big tractor is really something, ain't it?"

Which way to Machinery Hill? Seeing tractors parked in Minnesota's fields is a common sight—but one with twelve-foot wheels?

New York Mills Cultural Center, 24 Main Avenue North, (218) 385-3339. From Highway 10, go south on County Road 67 into town. The sculpture garden is along Highway 10.

While in the Area

After all the heady thoughts involved in a tour of New York Mills, hang your thinking cap at the Whistle Stop Inn, an original Pullman dining car from the early 1900s. The "Roaring Twenties" caboose has a little Murphy bed, and the "Private Palace Car" comes equipped with such modern luxuries as a whirlpool, a microwave, air conditioning, and a TV/VCR, as well as sleek mahogany paneling and floral carpet.

The Whistle Stop Inn, Route 1, Box 85, New York Mills, 56567, (218) 385-2223 or 1-800-328-6315.

Northwest Angle

Fort St. Charles

The Life of an Angle-ite

L iving in the northernmost point of the continental United States can make you a little loopy. The remote Northwest Angle pokes up above the rest of Minnesota and is accessible without crossing into Canada only by boat across Lake of the Woods. The border with our northern neighbors was set as the forty-ninth parallel, but little Fort St. Charles poked up in defiance. Rather than risk a fight, Canada let the remote fort remain in American hands.

Life in the wilderness is not for everyone. The locally published pamphlet *The Angler Guide to the Northwest Angle* states that you know you're an Angle-ite when:

- Dressing up is wearing store-bought clothes.
- You go cruising in a canoe.
- Live entertainment is watching bears at the dump.
- You have to kill your dinner before you eat it.
- You use pine sap for super glue.
- You prefer leaves over toilet paper.

The Northwest Angle's Magnusson Island contains a reconstruction of the walls of Fort St. Charles, built in 1732 by Pierre La Verendrye. The fort was the northern- and westernmost European settlement on the continent at the time and it was used as a trading post and a base for seeking a Northwest Passage. A log chapel sits next to the fort with a memorial to Father Jean Aulneau, who was killed by a group of Dakota in 1736. A small plaque commemorates the site with the words: "Headless bodies of Rev. Father Aulneau, J. B. LaVerendrye son of explorer."

Fort St. Charles in 1959, nine years after it was reconstructed by the Minnesota Fourth Degree Knights of Columbus.

Fort St. Charles. The most dramatic route to the fort is by boat from Baudette or Warroad across the huge Lake of the Woods. Otherwise, the dirt roads through Canada can be a little rough, unless, of course, you're an Angle-ite.

Olivia

Corn Capital

World Capital Intrigue

The politics of "World Capitals" is intense, especially when it comes to corn. In spite of having two seed companies, one canning factory, and the World's Largest Cornstalk, Olivia has bowed out of the competition and declared itself simply "the Corn Capital." After all, who can challenge the famous Corn Palace in Mitchell, South Dakota, with its fancy crop art walls and billboards every mile along I-90?

Even Olivia's claim to the largest corncob is in jeopardy, however, since Coon Rapids, Iowa, has announced plans to construct an ear of corn stretching fifty feet into the air. The jury's still out on whether Rochester's cornstalk-shaped water tower can truly enter the competition; after all, which came first, form or function? Corncob or water tower?

For centuries, Native Americans have raised communal plots of corn on the land around Olivia. Nowadays, pickups are parked everywhere, with their backs bursting with ears. Cornfields stretch for miles in every direction, with silos the only breaks in the skyline.

Olivia ignores the world capital controversy and stages its Corn Capital Days on the last weekend of July. Thousands of ears of corn are boiled up for free and the 2,600 Olivians sit down for a cornfeed.

Looming precariously on top of a cupola in Olivia's Memorial Park, the twelve-foot-tall corncob hails the harvest that put this town on the map.

As fans of the "Get Physical" singer Olivia Newton John, residents sparked a campaign to "Bring Olivia to Olivia." The singer obliged, jetted into town, and performed her hits during Corn Capital Days. All she asked for in payment was a couple dozen ears of corn.

Giant Ear of Corn. From downtown Olivia, drive west on Highway 212 until you see Memorial Park on the south side of the road.

Pelican Rapids

World's Largest Pelican

"A Part of All of Us"

"The pelican is a part of all of us, no matter how long we've lived here," said Truman Strand of the Pelican Committee in 1982. Standing fifteen and a half feet tall, the bird watches over the little waterfall at Mill Pond as trout playfully jump in the water at its feet.

In 1957, metalworkers Anton and Ted Resset were inspired to build the town symbol by a stuffed pelican they'd seen. An enormous cardboard mock-up was hastily cut out, and when it looked impressive enough, they pulled out their acetylene torches. Debate raged about whether to cover the steel frame in cement or fiberglass. In the end, the neorealists won out, arguing that cement looked more lifelike than fiberglass, and perhaps lasted longer to boot.

"The pelican was erected in 1957 at the urging of civic leaders," says the town's tourist literature. The large-beaked bird has a front-row seat to many bizarre festivals in the picturesque downtown park. In mid-July, Pelican Rapids holds a huge Turkey Festival, with specially constructed pits for cooking row upon row of turkeys on the spit. Turkeys that aren't cooked are raced in a heated competition.

Minnow races are also a regular event for children in the summer. Kids drop their "racing minnow" in a parallel gutter filled with water and hope their fish know the way to the other end. For the less advanced, worms are raced in front of the library. The uninterested worms are put in a circle and the first to the edge isn't bait. For adults, the annual Ugly Truck Contest in July is good for a few laughs, as you learn how junky and loud a pickup can get and still run.

Minnows and worms aside, the symbol of the town remains "The World's Largest Pelican," which is perched above the beginning of the Pelican River. Most businesses carry the name of the mascot: the Pelican Drug, the Pelican Motel (complete with a little pelican statue in front of it).

Since 1957, the World's Largest Pelican has been carefully watching over the waterfall in the heart of Pelican Rapids. The big cement bird sympathizes with its feathered brethren who are roasted for the annual Turkey Festival.

184 / Pelican Rapids

The coffee jerk at an espresso bar across the street from the statue laughed when asked if there were any live pelicans in town. "Ha ha! No, I think we chased all the pelicans out of town. You can't even find a duck around now!" he said. Nevertheless, Pelican Rapids celebrated the twenty-fifth anniversary of its emblem in 1982 with "The World's Largest Birthday Cake," measuring eighteen feet high—two and a half feet taller than the bird.

World's Largest Pelican. Pelican Rapids is twelve miles west of I-94 on Highway 108. The pelican guards the waterfall from Mill Pond at the beginning of the Pelican River at Highway 59 and West Mill Street.

Pequot Lakes

Paul Bunyan's Fishing Bobber
Relics of the Giant

The sky-blue water tower of Pequot Lakes looked like the water tower of any other town across the nation—until the city council voted to slosh gallons of red and white paint on it and declare their water tower Paul Bunyan's bobber. What some had considered a waterworks eyesore became a statue and a town symbol.

Other towns along the Paul Bunyan Trail hopped on the lumberwagon as well. With a lot of fiberglass and a little paint, villages erected their own monuments for tourist photo ops. Visitors to Ortonville now line up to shoot snapshots in front of Paul's 225,000-pound anchor by Big Stone Lake. At the headwaters of the Mississippi, Paul Bunyan's enormous wheelbarrow sits outside the Itasca Trading Post. Could this have been the water tanker that Babe the Blue Ox tipped over to form the Mississippi?

While other towns have built monuments to Paul Bunyan's earthly possessions, Kelliher attained the spiritual with the lumberjack's eternal resting place. Having left the material world for the mythological in 1899, Paul's forty-foot-long tomb is inscribed with the simple epitaph, "Here Lies Paul, And That's All." When the enormous Babe went to ox heaven, his physical remains were buried in South Dakota, forming the Black Hills.

Pequot Lakes cites an elaborate story about Paul's bobber penned by local revisionist historian, Jo McCarthy, who claims that Paul accepted a challenge to catch Notorious Nate the Northern out of Lake Whitefish. A Swedish blacksmith (who was, of course, named Ole) made a sixty-foot bobber, which was coincidentally just the size of a water tower. Paul's hook almost snagged Sunfish Sally, so Nate the forty-foot Northern swam into harm's way to save his beloved. Paul mustered all of his might to pull the snared northern pike and threw the fish seven miles away to Pequot Lakes. The bobber conveniently

The smashing success of Paul Bunyan's bobber in luring tourists to this fishing destination has area golf courses convinced that repainting the water tower as a golf ball would bring golfers to their greens.

landed in the braces built to hold a water tower, and the hole that Nate formed when he crashed to earth is used to this day to cook cauldrons of beans for the annual Beanhole Days. Ms. McCarthy explains that Sunfish Sally was so depressed at losing Nate that she became, ha ha, a "Blue Gill."

Even though nearly every tourist in the area gapes at the huge bobber overhead, dissidents have been talking about changing the water tower to look like a golf ball because of the many courses in the area. Paul Bunyan's golf ball? That's going too far.

"What do you mean, 'Paul Bunyan's grave'?" a group of guys in Kelliher respond when asked where the lumberjack's tomb lies. As they head into Thor's Sports Bar, they laugh, "You mean the poor guy's dead? Maybe you should come into Thor's and see a live band!" Luckily, Kelliher is small enough to find Paul Bunyan Memorial Park without their guidance, just south of downtown on Highway 72.

Paul Bunyan's Bobber. Pequot Lakes is thirty minutes north of Brainerd on Highway 371. The red-and-white bobber/water tower looms above the one stoplight in town, next to the highway.

While in the Area

Stop in early and often for the bumbleberry pie at Mary Etta's pie shop just east of town on Highway 11. Better show up by noon because the berry pies always sell out.

Paul Bunyan's old stomping grounds left a string of lakes around Pequot Lakes, and now a 48-mile loop of roads around the Whitefish Chain bears the name of the gentle giant.

Pine City

Perseverance the Voyageur
World's Largest Chainsaw Sculpture?

A ccording to interpretive displays in Pine City, people have been living along the banks of the Snake River since 6000 B.C. The Ojibwe named the area "Chengwatana," meaning "steep end of a spur of
hills"; settlers later called it just "Pine City."

A huge thirty-five-foot redwood log was transported into town in
the 1970s, but no one had the heart to chop up the beautiful lumber,
which came from an old-growth California forest. The wood changed
hands a few times and was finally carved into an enormous voyageur
and placed in Riverside Park to commemorate the first explorers in the
area. "We watched that sculptor from Hinckley carve it standing on a
cherry picker using all sorts of different-sized chainsaws," commented
Ryan, a resident of Pine City.

"We make sure that anybody who comes to visit us sees it," added his
wife, as they sat in their car admiring the impressive French-Canadian
voyageur. "We just think it's a great addition to our community."

Perseverance the Voyageur. From I-35, take the Pine City exit going
east. Drive through town, cross the Snake River, and look for the
voyageur statue on your left in Riverside Park.

While in the Area

West of downtown, the Minnesota Historical Society runs a replica of
an 1804 Northwest Company Fur Post that originally stood in the area
along the banks of the Snake River. Displays show how Indians taught
voyageurs to use birch bark canoes to run the first big business in the
state, the fur trade.

Northwest Company Fur Post, (612) 629-6356. Take the County
Road 7 exit off I-35 going west (away from Pine City). Drive about a

Pine City's thirty-five-foot-tall redwood voyageur is probably the World's
Largest Chainsaw Sculpture, so the appropriate title, "Perseverance," is
carved into the base in honor of pioneers' tenacity in weathering Minnesota's
winters and in carving the sculpture.

mile and look for signs on the right for the Northwest Company Fur Post. Summer only.

Just off I-35 at Rush City, a huge walleye pike gobbles up passing pickups and guards the Conoco Station convenience store as Winnebagos and Ford F-150s gas up for the trip to the lake. When the store manager was grilled about the World's Largest Walleye claim, she quickly backpedaled, repeating, "It's just a joke. It's just a joke." Another claim is that Paul Bunyan pulled this lunker out of nearby Rush Lake. Hey, they even have the stats to prove it:

Weight: 1999 pounds, 15 ½ ounces

Bait: 35-pound tiger muskie

Line: 1-inch manila rope

Rod: 62-foot white pine

Reel: 3-ton logger's winch

Ranier

Big Vic the Voyageur
The Protest Statue

The Feds were after Vic Davis. They wanted his island on Rainy Lake on the border with Canada as part of Voyageurs National Park. Davis wasn't about to give up his land without a fight, so he began selling off his land for $19.95 a square foot to his buddies in 1980. Hopefully, the federal government would get too bogged down finding all the landowners and let Davis keep Cranberry Island.

At the same time, he commissioned F.A.S.T. (Fiberglass Animals, Shapes, and Trademarks) in Sparta, Wisconsin, to make an enormous fiberglass voyageur to intimidate the Feds. Delivery was included in the purchase price, but Davis lived in one of the most remote areas of the state. The *Minneapolis Tribune* ran a story titled "Big Vic statue installed as land protest" in 1980, with an outstanding photo of the twenty-five-foot-tall voyageur dangling from a rope attached to a helicopter.

Unfortunately, the government struck back with bureaucracy, slapping a fine on the pilot for unintentionally wandering into Canadian airspace while searching for the border island. When their heavy-handed tactics further entrenched Davis, the Feds stormed the island one night, kicked him off his land, and took the 2,300-pound statue hostage.

The government was about to give the voyageur statue back to Vic when it discovered he was planning to erect it once again in protest. Instead, Davis was paid a nominal amount for the statue.

Although it looked like the law had won, Davis didn't give up hope. He couldn't muster up his own army to fight Uncle Sam, but he could get on the phone to Sparta and order another voyageur with the money from Washington. The good folks at F.A.S.T. were only too glad to comply. Rather than Big Vic II, the new voyageur was dubbed Big Louie in honor of Louie Reel, "a voyageur rebel in the 1800s," according to Davis.

He couldn't fly the new statue to his old island, so the 3,100-pound

"The protest voyageur" stands just west of International Falls at the entrance to the town of Ranier, with no description of its tumultuous past. "Vic is a rebel," claims the bartender in town, referring to Vic Davis's stance against the federal government's intrusion into privately owned land.

A less controversial voyageur stands at the end of State Route 24 at Crane Lake. From Orr, turn onto State Route 23 and drive for twenty-five miles into the wild toward Canada. Don't miss the town of Buyck (pronounced "bike") with its log-cabin post office. This paddle-carrying voyageur greets visitors with a plaque proclaiming, "The gay garb of these couragous [sic] happy men is typified by our memorial as he stands here proudly surveying the lands and waterways he once roamed."

fiberglass sculpture was plopped next to the visitors' center at Voyageurs National Park, peering down on the Feds. "U.S. Officials upset over Voyageurs Statue," blared the headline from the *Minneapolis Tribune* in 1982. Vic got wind that the government was itching to get their hands on the second fiberglass Goliath, too, so Big Louie went into hiding.

The twenty-five-foot statue resurfaced years later, when the threat of government confiscation had subsided. Davis decided to sell his voyageur, advertising it by saying "Big Louie is suitable as tourist attraction, lawn ornament, or government protest." The city of Barnum, half an hour south of Duluth, couldn't resist, and purchased the giant to lure tourists off I-35.

The U.S. District Court eventually awarded Davis $90,000 payment for Cranberry Island, and the government donated Big Vic to the city of Ranier, where he stands at the intersection of Highways 332 and 11. No

Other entrances to Voyageurs National Park feature roadside sculpture to lure adventurers into the wilderness. At the intersection of Highway 53 and State Route 122, tourists saddle up on Kabetogama's walleye for a photo to show the folks back home how big the fish are up north.

mention is made of the struggle behind the giant. Local revisionist historians claim its name is not Big Vic, but that it is instead named after the founder of the first voyageur outpost in Ranier in 1788. Vic Davis's mother thinks differently: "You can tell them they're full of hot air! The statue is named 'Big Vic' and don't let them tell you otherwise!"

Big Vic the Voyageur. From International Falls, go east on Highway 11 about three miles. The statue is at the entrance to the town of Ranier.

Redwood Falls

Lower Sioux Agency Historic Site

"Let Them Eat Grass!"

Times were tough in 1862. A drought had killed crops across southwestern Minnesota, and a famine seemed inevitable. Native Americans living in that area went to the Lower Sioux Agency near Redwood Falls to claim money and grain from the warehouses that was owed to them as part of the Treaty of Travers.

"Let them eat grass!" the head of the agency supposedly told the Native Americans after they requested food in exchange for their credit. His refusal to open the storehouses caused a group of outraged young Dakota to convince their elders to condone an attack on the agency on August 20, 1862. The corpse of the head agent, Myrick, was later found with his mouth stuffed with grass.

This Minnesota Historical Society site charts these events and features displays of Dakota culture in the area. A recently restored stone warehouse sits on the site next to a teepee to give a feel for the old days, when this was a gathering area rather than a battlefield.

Inside the interpretive center, an exhibition shows how the uprising spread downriver to Fort Ridgely near Fairfax, where the Dakota were held back by 180 soldiers. New Ulm was a target of repeated attacks, and one of Minnesota's most famous doctors, W. W. Mayo, was on hand there to treat the wounded. When the dust settled, three hundred whites had been killed in the uprising; no one ever bothered counting the number of dead Native Americans.

A copy of President Abraham Lincoln's approval of a list of thirty-nine Indians (one of whom was later granted a reprieve) to be hanged in Mankato is displayed. The original roster included 392 Dakota who were put on trial by November 5, but even the trimmed back list contained two cases of mistaken identity. A large photo in the museum portrays the teepees of 1,600 prisoners held at Fort Snelling.

For the hanging, alcohol was banned for two days for fifteen miles

197

around Mankato. Fourteen hundred infantry were called up to guard the prisoners and to prevent a riot. A special gallows was prepared to hang all the Dakota at the same time, but the rope wouldn't break. Some viewed this as a sign the convicted should be set free, but William Duley, whose family members had been killed in the uprising, slashed it with his pocket knife to execute the thirty-eight, making it the largest mass execution in U.S. history.

According to *The Sioux Uprising of 1862* by Kenneth Carley, "The dead were buried in a single shallow grave near the riverfront. That night several doctors, quick to seize the rare opportunity to obtain subjects for anatomical study, dug up the bodies. Dr. Mayo drew that of Cut Nose, and later his sons learned osteology from the Indian's skeleton."

In honor of the Native Americans who had helped shelter settlers from the battles, nearby Morton erected a controversial statue to "The Friendly Indians." These included John Other Day and others who had converted to Christianity and accepted the ways of the whites.

The Lower Sioux Agency Historic Site clarifies the tragic events of 1862 and gives an illuminated history of the Dakota in Minnesota.

Lower Sioux Agency Historic Site. From downtown Redwood Falls, take Highway 19 east, but turn right on County Road 2 before crossing the Minnesota River and follow the signs.

Redwood Falls

Minnesota Inventors Hall of Fame
Puffing Cannons to Pacemakers

Eccentric designers from across the state converge on Redwood Falls every June for the Minnesota Inventors Congress, filling up the high school gymnasium with everything from handy-dandy gadgets to Happy-to-Be-Me dolls. Winners inducted into the Minnesota Inventors Hall of Fame have their plaques proudly displayed at the Redwood County Museum (formerly the poorhouse).

Although the musty museum concentrates more on county history than inventors and less on the inventions than on the awards, the two-room display illuminates Minnesotan creativity and practicality.

Daniel F. Przhylski, for example, earned forty-four patents for ditch digging. Harold Stabenau designed a lever-lock window handle that "changed forever the future of Truth Tool Co. of Mankato." Another inventor, Henry Buchwald, escaped Nazi persecution to come to Minnesota and concoct the Double Chamber Multi Micro Orifice Collector, as well as the useful Peritoneovenous Shunts and an Implantable Glucose Sensor.

Slightly more recognizable innovations are featured in the women inventors room. "Bounce" was created by Minnesotan Alice McQueary in 1976. "Scotch-Gard" came to light when Patsy Sherman accidentally spilled a chemical on a tennis shoe and couldn't wash it off. No solvents would remove the mystery mixture, and her miracle formula caused a splash on the market.

Another odd chemical concoction was derived by Allene R. Jeanes in 1962 for "industrial uses such as film formation as thickeners or bodying agents for edible compositions, cosmetic formulations, pharmaceutical vehicles and drilling muds." In other words, her "gum polymer derivative" could be used in your favorite beauty creams and snack products. Products using her secret recipe are displayed, including Duncan Hines desserts and bottles of barbecue sauce.

Bette Graham was a struggling artist working as a frustrated secretary when she stumbled across her real destiny as an inventor. Using her kitchen hand mixer, she stirred up secret ingredients into a chalky white solution to correct her typing blunders. This "Liquid Paper" blend was funneled into little bottles by her son, Michael Nesmith, who later left town for an aspiring career with the Monkees.

Besides the work of these famous inventors, a section of the museum features the life of Richard W. Sears. Working on the railroad in Redwood Falls in 1886, Sears noticed a box of watches lying unclaimed at the depot, so he hawked the fancy timepieces riding the rails of the

Just west of Redwood Falls, the county poorhouse has been transformed into the county museum and home of the Minnesota Inventors Hall of Fame. Next to large weapons displays and a fake meteor, such visionaries as LeRoy Buffington (who patented his Iron Building Construction) and Carl Kronmiller (the inventor of Time-O-State Controls) are heralded for their brainstorms.

Minneapolis & St. Louis Railroad. Later that year, he moved up to the Twin Cities to open the Sears Watch Company, but soon moved to Chicago looking for a watchmaker. Perhaps having seen the success of St. Paul–based G. Sommers & Co.'s mail-order business, Sears hooked up with Alvah Roebuck. The rest is history.

Redwood County Museum, (507) 637-3329 or (507) 637-2828. From downtown Redwood Falls, take Highway 19 west and look for the signs to the Redwood County Museum. Summer only.

Roseau

Polaris Snowmobile Tours

Iron Dogs on Ice

Edgar and Allan Hetteen and their buddy David Johnson were tired of cross-country skiing and snowshoeing to their favorite wilderness spots in the thick of winter. Sure, it was good exercise and perhaps peaceful, but they knew there was a better way.

David Johnson, one of the cofounders of Polaris, takes a breather before risking life and limb venturing into the forest to chop wood. This archival photo from 1959 shows a "Sno-Traveler," one of the earliest snowmobiles pieced together by Johnson and Edgar and Allan Hetteen.

Their company, Polaris in Roseau, had been set up to make farm machinery in 1954, so they gathered a pile of old mechanical parts and got to work. The entrepreneurs tacked a little engine running a tread on some skis and soon their clunky "iron dogs" sputtered through the snow to their amazement. The first snowmobiles were born.

What began as a dangerous experiment to zoom on top of the snow has become a tourist boom for the northwoods. One in every twenty residents of Minnesota now owns a snowmobile—the most in the country. In 1995, 217,708 snowmobiles were registered in the state to use the 14,000 miles of snowmobile trails, once again, the most in the nation. Trails extend all the way to the Upper Peninsula of Michigan, up to Winnipeg and across Ontario.

Soon other companies, like Arctic Cat in nearby Thief River Falls, hopped on the bandwagon. Polaris now offers tours of its factory and plans are underway for a snowmobile museum and restaurant in an abandoned Land-O-Lakes creamery next to the factory. Although Polaris may not have the first snowmobile ever built, the #2 sled is on the grounds, and aficionados have been eager to lend collectible "iron dogs" for the world to see in the snowmobile museum. The Roseau County Historical Society also has a large collection of snowmobile artifacts.

Polaris, 301 Fifth Avenue SW, (218) 463-2312. From Highway 11, turn south on Highway 89 (Fifth Avenue) until Third Street SW and look for the signs. Roseau County Historical Society, 110 Second Avenue NE, (218) 463-1918.

Rothsay

World's Largest Prairie Chicken
Nine-Thousand-Pound Fertility Charm

Rothsay needed a town symbol, something to represent the proud, hardworking farmers of this haven on the Great Plains. The prairie chicken seemed like the obvious choice after "a guest speaker at a meeting of the Agassiz Study Club just happened to mention that the bird was native to the area," according to historian Karal Ann Marling.

Rothsay tourist brochures describe how "[p]rairie chickens moved ahead of the settlers to inhabit the prairies of Minnesota." Just as the birds had cleared the way for the pioneers, the town broke new ground by officially declaring itself the Prairie Chicken Capital of Minnesota on June 10, 1975.

Sculptor Art Fosse was given the green light and began bending steel pipes for the bird's ribs and slapping on thousands of pounds of cement. He had studied the bird's habits and chose to depict the bizarre mating ritual of the male, which involves strutting around making booming noises while spreading its wings and puffing up its unusual orange air sac. The result was a sort of nine-thousand-pound fertility symbol.

The "Booming Prairie Chicken" was unveiled to the world on June 15, 1976, with a front-page photo in the *Minneapolis Tribune*. The purpose of the chicken was "to alert area visitors and remind local residents of the beauty to be found on the native prairie grasslands," according to the base of the statue.

This roadside attraction stands above I-94 and was unintentionally designed with its beak resting at the perfect height for photos showing it pecking some poor soul's head.

Booming Prairie Chicken. Rothsay is about twenty-five miles north of Fergus Falls on I-94. The chicken is visible from the interstate.

Sneaking out before dawn and hiding in chicken blinds is a spring tradition on the prairie. As the sun rises, the booming prairie chickens rustle in the underbrush and the males begin to show off. For the next couple of hours, bizarre noises emerge from these birds as they puff up their unusual orange air sacs and strut around to claim their territory.

Royalton

Treasure City

Minnesota's Wall Drug

Rising up above a flat stretch of Highway 10 is a two-dimensional pirate luring travelers into his treasure cove. Flags in every color of the rainbow adorn the lime-green building and lawn ornaments guard the grass around this jewel-filled Mecca.

Discover the riches within the walls of this souvenir paradise along Highway 10, such as wind chimes, plastic Indian spears, and small cedar chests inscribed with clever quotations.

For years I begged whoever was driving to please stop the car so I could enter this tourist paradise. Finally, when I was eight years old, my grandfather gave in to the kicking and screaming and pulled his pale blue Oldsmobile into the parking lot of Treasure City. I was so excited I had to go to the bathroom right away.

With that emergency averted, Grandpa declared, "Choose a souvenir, anything you want!" My jaw dropped as I looked around at all the arrowheads, plastic tomahawks, backscratchers, and fool's gold. "This could take a while," I responded. After searching through all the bins, I decided on a neon-green rabbit's foot, hoping it would bring me enough luck to return to this fantasyland.

Bob Janski founded Treasure City in 1961 after seeing the success of other tourist wayside rests, like South of the Border and the Wisconsin Dells. With legions of boaters passing by Royalton and rarely stopping, he needed something to lure them off the roaring highway. Borrowing the idea of free ice water from Wall Drug in South Dakota, he persuaded thirsty vacationers to pull over for a sip. Of course the thirty-foot-tall signs also helped to seduce bored urchins into this knickknack nirvana.

Treasure City has changed little since its inception. The shelves are still loaded with lava lamps, little shell waterfalls that light up, bins of agates, and shot glasses printed with drinking witticisms. The big pirate out front has grown from a Disney's Captain Hook look-alike to a huge scowling Long John Silver. Although the color has been updated from the green and pastel yellow of the 1960s to fire-engine red, backseat brats can still have their dreams come true—but they probably now prefer Beanie Babies to lucky rabbit's feet.

Treasure City, 308 North Highway 10, (320) 584-5140. Take Highway 10 north of St. Cloud about twenty miles and look for the huge signs for Treasure City in Royalton, next to the highway.

St. Louis Park

Pavek's Museum of Wonderful Wireless
"What Hath God Wrought?"

Ever since Samuel Morse sent the weighty words, "What hath God wrought?" in the first Morse code message of 1844, the communications world has never been the same.

The Pavek Museum of Broadcasting incorporates four different radio collections, charting the history of broadcasting since Morse's famous phrase and James Clerk Maxwell's discovery in 1865 of a relationship between the waves of electricity and sound signals. Reginald Aubrey Fessenden of Canada took Maxwell's theory and created the first wireless in 1906. When voices were transmitted to ships, many radio operators thought their controls were haunted and that their radios were possessed by sirens of the sea.

Scores of old radio sets line the walls of the museum, as well as a huge Tesla coil "amplifier" that looks more like a drying rack for clothes. Also displayed are the strange antenna hats and shoes the military used to rig the human body with cable to receive transmissions before the invention of portable radios.

A collection of old phonographs is exhibited, as well as an example of Edison's first phonograph of tinfoil wrapped around a drum from 1928. Edison stubbornly claimed that the sound of his drums was far superior to these newfangled "turntables."

The Twin Cities also contributed to the broadcasting world with sixty different radio builders; by 1928 only a handful survived. Unfortunately, most of these manufacturers didn't survive until the 1939 New York World's Fair, when different color radio sets were finally introduced.

The Minnesota collection of the museum features photos of the old "Barn Dance" show, which topped the charts locally in the 1940s as a precursor to *Hee-Haw*. The curators are also quick to point out that

Neon Motorola signs illuminate RCA Victor's quizzical dog at Pavek's museum, where an immense collection of radios and televisions stuns the crowds of children who visit every year.

"The Pavek Museum is the only place in the world where you can get videos of the locally-produced 'Axel and His Dog Show.'"

WCCO's very first microphone and huge old camera cranes from KSTP and WCCO give the feel of a real television station to the game show background that is the highlight for the four thousand kids who visit each year. The hypothetical possibility of winning $64,000 and the unusual homespun radios make the Pavek Museum "the most popular destination for school field trips," according to the curators.

Pavek Museum of Broadcasting, 3515 Raleigh Avenue, St. Louis Park, (952) 926-8198. From I-394, turn on Highway 100 going south. Turn off on County Road 25 going east (look for Byerly's supermarket), until Ottawa Avenue South, which becomes Belt Line Boulevard. Turn right, go across the railroad tracks to West Thirty-Fifth Street, which becomes Raleigh Avenue, and look for the big antennas.

St. Paul

El Dorado Conquistador Collection
Black Velvet to Hardened Foam

"It all began over at the West Bank School of Music when I found a foam conquistador head," recalls Scott Wentworth. Without a university degree in art, Wentworth has assembled one of the strangest anti-art exhibits in the country, comparable only to the Museum of Bad Art in Boston.

Wentworth's obsession led him to Salvation Armies across the state, where he scoured for tacky Spanish-style kitsch last seen in shag-floored rec rooms of the late 1960s. He patently refused to pass his two-dollar limit per objet d'art in his quest for beauty. Brass plates with Spanish galleons, black velvet matadors, velour versions of Rembrandt's *Man with the Golden Helmet,* and painted foam reliefs of conquistadors soon filled his house. The collection accompanied his band, Full Metal Hangover, to gigs at seedy Minneapolis clubs, where they would whip out a cover of the "Different Strokes" theme song.

A fellow "curator" and drinking buddy unearthed a huge five-headed conquistador at Goodwill, but the price tag was a whopping fifteen dollars, far over budget. He tenderly placed it in his cart to think for a minute, but other bargain hunters kept asking him if he was going to buy it. Realizing it was now or never, he plunked down his last cash and dragged the huge foam relief two miles home. The proud curator changed his tone when calling up his sweetheart to explain that he wasn't feeling well and couldn't go out that night. Co-curator Wentworth heaped praise on him for doing the right thing: choosing art over love. His girlfriend, however, thought otherwise.

Inspired by a well-stocked fridge of beer, Wentworth invented origins for his treasures—often involving Nazi art thieves, Sotheby's auction house, and Xanadu, the Foam House of Tomorrow—written on slick tags for each masterpiece. The new five-headed piece was named "The Graduating Class: Pizarro, Cortez, Ponce DeLeon, De Soto, and

This strange anti-art collection treats recycled mass-produced paintings and foam conquistador heads as precious valuables.

Columbus in search of El Dorado, the legendary city of simulated gold."

This treatment of cheesy paint-by-number knickknacks has landed the "museum" on the pages of local newspapers and the airwaves of public radio. "Imperialism has never been so chic. . . . You can almost smell the blood," raved *Minnesota Law and Politics* in 1998. Upon hearing this hype, an outraged ex–elementary school teacher stomped into the museum, questioning this "revisionist history" and insisting, "The conquistadors were explorers, not killers!"

Curator Scott Wentworth hasn't swayed from his artistic vision of portraying kitsch as precious, embellishing with his usual sarcasm, "They're priceless; they have no price."

El Dorado Conquistador Collection, 875 Summit Avenue, (651) 290-6378. Take the Lexington Avenue exit south off I-94. At Summit Avenue turn left. The museum is on the northwest corner of Victoria and Summit in the basement of the William Mitchell Law School. (Would alum and Chief Justice Warren Burger have approved?)

St. Paul

Forepaugh and Griggs Mansions

Haunted Houses

Seeing St. Paul's old Victorian mansions inevitably leads to tales of murder, treachery, and troubled ghosts. The Ramsey County Courthouse, the Landmark Center, and even the State Capitol are supposedly haunted (maybe Rudy Perpich is seeking revenge). The most impressive haunted house, however, is the majestic and macabre Forepaugh mansion, located on the edge of Irvine Park, a Victorian-looking square once used as a backdrop by Italian horror film director Dario Argento.

Joseph Lybrandt Forepaugh built the house in 1870 next door to the house of Alexander Ramsey, the first territorial governor of Minnesota. The Ramsey House, at 265 Exchange Street, offers tours by straitlaced costumed guides who refuse to talk politics or religion with women, in keeping with the times.

In 1886, Alexander Ramsey paid a visit to Forepaugh's huge estate sale of almost everything in the house—"the finest sale of house-hold goods ever made in the Northwest," according to the auctioneers. The entire family was moving to Europe, allegedly to cure Joseph Forepaugh of melancholy; perhaps Minnesota winters had taken their toll. The house was sold to the man who had been chief of staff to General Sherman during the Civil War (who was thought to later haunt the building).

Forepaugh returned to St. Paul in 1889 and was found dead soon afterward next to a pond near "the Selby Avenue bridge over the Milwaukee railroad bridge," wrote the *St. Paul Pioneer Press* in 1892. "A bullet wound in the head and the revolver still clasped in the dead man's hand clearly indicated suicide." The strange subtitle of the article stated, "He found peace." Little did the reporter know that Forepaugh's ghost would come back to haunt his house.

The Italianate mansion has since been turned into a fancy French restaurant, but ghosts continually disturb table settings and scare the wait staff. "We'll blow out all the candles, and we'll come back and they'll all be lit," a terrified waitress said.

"One night, I was putting on my lipstick all alone," she said. "Then I looked in the mirror and behind me a single clothes hanger was moving. I don't believe in ghosts, but there was just an overwhelming feeling. This really bothered me."

A séance in 1998 revealed one of the ghosts to be Molly, the maid who had been Forepaugh's mistress. When he moved away, she was left

"The most notoriously haunted house in St. Paul," according to the *St. Paul Pioneer Press*, but its owner claims, "It's all stories." Whatever you believe, the history of the Griggs mansion—fires, séances, and decadent parties—has to make you wonder.

behind, and she promptly committed suicide. "You can still smell her perfume," said the waitress. "It's lilac or one of those Victorian scents."

Forepaugh's Restaurant, 276 South Exchange Street, (651) 224-5606. From I-94 eastbound, take the Fifth Street exit to West Seventh Street (Highway 5). Turn right and drive to Walnut Street. Take a left and the street leads into Irvine Park.

Griggs Mansion

"No, there's never been a problem here. It's all stories," says a man with a heavy Eastern European accent who opens the door at the enormous Griggs mansion on elegant Summit Avenue. They may be just stories, but there are enough of them to make the *Pioneer Press* write in 1982, "The house at 476 Summit Avenue may be the most notoriously haunted house in St. Paul."

The Romanesque limestone house was built by grocery tycoon Chauncey W. Griggs in 1883. The ceilings are twelve feet high on the first floor and tower to forty feet in the third-floor ballroom. The marble fireplaces all have cast-iron hearths; the marble mantle in the library even portrays an eerie cockfight. After years of construction, Griggs lived in the house for only four years before he mysteriously moved out.

Following an unexplained fire in 1910, the ghost of the gardener, Charles Wade, could sometimes be seen browsing through the books of the huge library that went up in smoke.

In subsequent years, the house changed hands many times until it was donated to the St. Paul School of Art, which used it for many years for classrooms and studios.

The following owner made the house the home of the nation's largest occult book publisher, Llewellyn Press, which didn't help dispel the house's reputation for ghosts. The walls were painted red with "gloomy illumination," according to a pamphlet written about the house. The second floor was covered with metallic wallpaper called both "pornographic" and "psychic" by later owners. An L-shaped room was created on the second floor for "psychic sessions and séances . . . it housed some rather unusual social activities," according to the discreet pamphlet.

Psychic Roma Harris once toured the house and said that she saw a Civil War–era officer decked out in a fancy blue uniform and a young girl named Amy who plays the piano.

The present owner insists there haven't been problems recently, then he cracks a smirk and adds, "but when the kids come around on Halloween, I'll tell them stories!"

Griggs Mansion, 476 Summit Avenue (private residence). From I-94 take the Dale Street exit south to Summit Avenue. Turn left and keep your eyes open for the mansion with the huge skylight on the right side of the road before Summit veers left.

While in the Area

Just up the street from the Griggs mansion is the elegant rowhouse at 599 Summit Avenue where author F. Scott Fitzgerald penned *This Side of Paradise,* published in 1920. The playboy author of *The Great Gatsby* coined the term "jazz age" and used to make merry in White Bear Lake with his wife, Zelda, before they moved on to greener pastures.

On the other side of Summit, at the end of Selby Avenue toward downtown, the James J. Hill House (240 Summit Avenue, [651] 297-2555) sits atop Cathedral Hill, overlooking the city. Funded by profits from the Great Northern Railroad, the "robber baron's" mansion was finished in 1891 with thirty-two rooms, thirteen bathrooms, and twenty-two fireplaces. The red sandstone building used to house the Minnesota Historical Society, which now offers tours.

To dine in the elegance of old St. Paul, stop in the pricey W. A. Frost (374 Selby Avenue, [651] 224-5715) at the corner of Selby and Western, especially if the beautiful patio is open. Kitty-corner from the restaurant is the more moderate Chatterbox Bar, where playwright August Wilson spent long hours writing *Fences* and other plays.

Over on Western is the Commodore Hotel (79 Western Avenue North, [651] 227-1400), with its elegant art nouveau lounge. Up Selby Avenue a few blocks are other classy but affordable restaurants in old brick buildings with patios: The Vintage (579 Selby Avenue, [651] 222-7000), and Chang O'Hara's, with a strange Irish-Chinese motif (498 Selby Avenue, [651] 290-2338). Across the parking lot from Chang O'Hara's is the St. Paul Curling Club (470 Selby Avenue, [651] 224-7408), where world-class sweepers melt the ice before their stones.

St. Paul

Gangster Tours

Ma Barker, Baby Face Nelson, and Alvin "Creepy" Karpis

Ever since Pierre "Pig's Eye" Parrant set up shop as a French-Canadian whiskey runner on the banks of the Mississippi River, the image of Minnesota's capital has been corrupt. In 1840, Father Lucien Galtier tried to purify the settlement by building a log chapel next to Pig's Eye's bar in honor of the apostle Paul. Galtier succeeded in renaming the town Saint Paul, but its holy moniker couldn't clean up its reputation.

Crime from Chicago overflowed north to St. Paul during the 1910s. Police Chief John O'Connor tried to reach a truce with the gangsters by letting them stay in St. Paul as long as they obeyed the rules of the city. No guns were allowed and laws gainst petty crime were strictly enforced. In exchange, the likes of "Machine Gun" Kelly and "Baby Face" Nelson would not be touched while in the city limits, even if the Feds had a warrant. With a nickname of "home safe home," St. Paul was a vacation destination for criminals, a place to hang their hats while things cooled down.

This questionable bargain backfired just as O'Connor retired and Prohibition was enacted. The Mississippi became a highway for moonshine from Canada going south, and St. Paul was the first big stop. Murders, bank robberies, and shoot-outs became all too common as the cops cracked down on these criminals.

One notorious underworld kingpin, Isadore "Kid Cann" Blumenfeld, began his career in the 1920s as a bootlegger from Canada to Minneapolis and Chicago, and he continued in the liquor trade for years. The FBI claimed that he controlled every liquor license issued in Minneapolis and St. Paul and was slipped up to $20,000 from each establishment for protection. As leader of "the Minneapolis Syndicate" or the "Minneapolis Combination," he was charged with three murders, but acquitted each time.

Pack your bathtub gin and meet at the Wabasha Street Caves (site of a gangland massacre in 1934) for a tour of St. Paul's most notorious gangster hot spots.

Minneapolis mayor Hubert Humphrey swore he'd expose his racket in 1945, but he only succeeded in forcing Kid Cann underground, since the city council was soaked in Cann's bribes. J. Edgar Hoover ranted that Cann was "a top hoodlum, to be the subject of a concerted all-out effort designed to effect a penetration of hoodlum activities." Kid Cann was untouchable in the Twin Cities, especially when he "went legit" in the 1950s.

For his final exploit, he hooked up with Twin City Rapid Transit president Fred Ossanna to loot the remaining assets of the TCRT, torch the Twin Cities' trolleys, and form the American Iron and Supply Company to cash in on the metal scrap from streetcars.

Enough time has now passed to make these and other bloody events a tourist attraction rather than a mar on the cities' images. St. Paul Gangster Tours leads guests around town with guides dressed in 1930s zoot suits. The excursion usually begins in the Wabasha Street Caves, where a massacre occurred in 1934 when it was the Castle Royale nightclub. Legend has it that the ghosts of the dead still haunt the cave.

The tour uncovers all the old hideouts and speakeasies of Prohibition-era St. Paul. See the rather ordinary-looking apartment building on Lexington Avenue where John Dillinger shot it out with the cops and fled. Walk into the post office where the Barker Gang pulled off the Swift Payroll Robbery. Hear how local boy George Moran became a gangster, too.

Before embarking on the tour, stop at the local independent bookstore to pick up a copy of *Saint Mudd* by Steve Thayer about St. Paul's sordid past and Paul Maccabee's *John Dillinger Slept Here,* a guide to the city's gangster hotspots. Even though the streets of St. Paul often seem painfully quiet now, these tours and books show there's still a little "Pig's Eye" bubbling beneath the surface.

Down in History Tours, 215 Wabasha Street, (651) 292-1220. Tours usually leave from the Wabasha Street Caves at 215 South Wabasha Street and Plato (or sometimes from the St. Paul Hotel). Call for details. From May 1 to November 1.

St. Paul

The God of Peace
Onyx John

Stepping off the busy streets of downtown St. Paul into the courthouse is a time warp into the city's art deco past. Two stories of dark blue Belgian marble and yellow strip lights rise up and then appear to continue two more because of the mirrored ceiling. At the end of the hall stands "The God of Peace," also known as Onyx John, carved from sixty tons of white quartz and the stunning crown jewel of city hall.

While the "God of Peace" statue is considered a masterpiece by many, other sculptures of Indians around the state have been criticized for being "offensive." The debate is strangely subjective. An Indian chief statue from the 1950s once greeted tourists as they entered the Mystery Cave in southeastern Minnesota, and supposedly even local Winnebago Indians from Albert Lea named him "Chief Decorah." When the caves became part of the state park system, the park manager thought the statue might offend Native American visitors, so the nearby Spring Valley tourist information center picked it up. I recently saw a group of Japanese tourists snapping photos of it.

An important factor in determining whether a statue is offensive seems to be its material. The valuable onyx of St. Paul's "God of Peace" stands in contrast to the fiberglass Indians of Battle Lake and the Thunderbird Hotel in Bloomington. Bemidji's recycled fiberglass Native American statue, supposedly of Nanabojo, was once a muffler man advertising sculpture, transformed with a little red paint.

Numerous chainsaw Indian chiefs across the state are criticized as objectionable, but sculptor Peter Toth was careful to list his Indian chainsaw sculpture in Two Harbors as "a gift to the people of Minnesota," designed to raise awareness of the plight of the "original Americans." With this disclaimer, he wisely deflects any criticism and possibly gains support for his dream of putting a similar monument in every state.

With mirrors overhead, yellow lights shooting up two stories, and dark Belgian marble all around, the "God of Peace" sculpture in the St. Paul City Hall is the high point of the art deco building.

Swedish sculptor Carl Milles probably didn't have to worry about this type of commentary when he carved "The God of Peace" in 1932. Of course he didn't promote his artwork as roadside sculpture or call it the World's Tallest Indian Statue—which it could very well be.

"God of Peace," St. Paul City Hall and Courthouse, 15 West Kellogg Boulevard. From I-94 eastbound, take the Fifth Street exit, then turn right on West Seventh Street. Turn left on the next block, Kellogg Boulevard. Follow it past the Xcel Energy Center and look for the art deco courthouse on the left between St. Peter and Wabasha.

St. Paul

Iggy the Lizard
The Science Museum's Mascot

Fifteen-year-old Nick Swearer brought an iguana home from school one day in a milk carton. He became completely enthralled with Spot the lizard, so much so that he lugged home more than twelve thousand railroad spikes from the train tracks near his Northfield home. He placed Spot on a pedestal, pulled out his acetylene torch, and began welding. Every day after school for four years, the sparks flew in his driveway as the neighbors peered out from behind the curtains to see what was going on at the Swearer house.

Just when Iggy the lizard was starting to take shape, Nick looked out his window and his masterpiece was missing. The iron giant couldn't be hidden for long, and turned up on the campus of Carleton College. According to Nick, as quoted in the *Pioneer Press,* "They must have been some college students. They carried him a mile. He only weighed a ton at the time, but I had to come and retrieve him. It cost me five days of work."

Iggy was bought for ten thousand dollars by art patrons Betty and John Musser, who donated him to the Science Museum of Minnesota in St. Paul. Recent renovation of the sculpture nearly doubled the original price tag. The nearly four-thousand pound, forty-foot-long sculpture has become the symbol of the museum and a jungle gym for visiting urchins. "I never put a coating on him," Swearer said to the *Pioneer Press.* "He is oiled by human oil, and he would be a red rust if he were not touched so much. It's the best compliment I can get. It shows how much people love him."

Once past the guarding iguana, the Science Museum is packed with hands-on exhibits. Not for the squeamish, the "Bloodstream Superhighway" wraps one hundred feet of tube pumping blood-red liquid in every nook and cranny of the Human Body Gallery. Play God by creating your own weather system and then make "wiggly waves with a

Lariat chain" in the experiment gallery. Move over, Creature from the Black Lagoon: short films at the 3D Laser Show enter into the brain, oceans, and ecosystems. And the many dinosaur skeletons are a favorite with all ages. After these carnivalesque scenes, relax in the Mississippi River Gallery and learn about the locks and dams while admiring a fantastic view of the mighty river.

Science Museum of Minnesota, 120 West Kellogg Boulevard, (651) 221-9444. From I-94 eastbound, take the Fifth Street exit, then turn right on West Seventh Street. Turn left on the next block, Kellogg Boulevard. Follow it past the Xcel Energy Center and look for the new glass building on your right. Iggy stands guard along the waterfront. Parking is available in the museum's ramp, which is built into the bluff

Teenage sculptor Nick Swearer welded more than twelve thousand railroad spikes in his Northfield driveway to create Iggy the Lizard, who now keeps watch in front of the Science Museum of Minnesota.

underneath the museum. To get to the ramp entrance, veer right immediately after you turn onto Kellogg, *before* you pass the Xcel Energy Center. Signs will direct you down the hill and to the left, where you can enter the ramp.

While in the Area

The Minnesota Children's Museum is every kid's dream, with a "Habitot" play space for babies and toddlers, and galleries filled with opportunities for dramatic play and scientific discovery. Favorite areas include a Korean restaurant, a fluids laboratory (complete with boats and ping-pong balls), and a nature gallery where kids can create their own thunderstorms. Adults only wish they could play along, squeezing into the anthill mazes and taking a turn operating the electromagnetic crane.

Minnesota Children's Museum, 10 West Seventh Street, (651) 225-6000. From I-94, take the Tenth Street exit into downtown. Turn right on St. Peter Street, then go two blocks to West Seventh Street and turn

Jerry O'Mahoney, Inc., of New Jersey loaded up a flatbed train with a yellow-and-red dining car diner in 1939, bound west. When the locomotive arrived in St. Paul, the diner was named Mickey's and it has supposedly been open every day since. Mickey's Diner, 36 West Seventh Street, (651) 222-5633.

left. Reduced rate parking is available at the museum's ramp at the corner of West Seventh and Wabasha Streets, kitty-corner from the museum.

If Mickey's Diner isn't what the doctor ordered for lunch, venture across the Wabasha Street Bridge away from downtown to Harriet Island. Down on the docks, the No Wake Café serves up American cooking on a boat. The No Wake was once more of a houseboat, so brash boaters making waves caused your lunch to shake around (thus the name). Now after renovation the boat doesn't jiggle, and a few rooms are available as a B & B.

Mickey's Diner, 36 West Seventh Street, (651) 222-5633. No Wake Café and the Covington Inn, Pier 1, Harriet Island, (651) 292-1411. No Wake Café open summer only.

St. Paul

Jackson Street Railroad Roundhouse
Hub of "The Largest Railway in the World"

In 1862, the first locomotive maintenance center in the state was set up on Jackson Street, a sure sign that Minnesota was moving into the modern era. The Minnesota & Pacific Railroad soon changed its name to the St. Paul & Pacific Railroad, but ended up declaring bankruptcy in 1879.

Enter James J. Hill, "The Empire Builder." He bought the floundering company, renaming it the St. Paul, Minneapolis, & Manitoba Railroad. Hill was able to form the largest railway system in the world at the time, which eventually evolved into the Great Northern Railroad.

He wielded his power mercilessly, threatening to bypass Minnesota towns unless they gave him free prime real estate. The town of Wayzata finally surrendered to Hill's tactics, knowing that having no railroad connection was suicide, and donated prime downtown Lake Minnetonka property to Hill. No wonder his nickname of "railroad baron" was usually altered to "robber baron."

In spite of the highway's manifest destiny, the Minnesota Transportation Museum was able to salvage the Jackson Street Roundhouse in 1987 and renovate it for a museum, offices, and railcar restoration shop. The railway stopped using the building in 1959, but a few vintage railroad cars are on display and more are slated to be restored in the near future.

All aboard a restored Duluth/South Shore & Atlantic railroad car! Peruse paintings of locomotives with lone cowboys saluting the iron beasts. See the Soo Line that crisscrossed the state.

Inside the museum, climb a "Cow Catcher" scoop hooked onto the front of engines to bulldoze anything in their paths. Witness photos of horrible railway derailments. You can even buy a video of terrible train wrecks! And, finally, the origin of the "choo-choo" sound is revealed.

Tour guides' verve for all things on iron rails makes visitors believe

The old caboose greets guests at the Jackson Street Roundhouse. Inside the museum, a 1910 caboose is displayed, complete with cots, oil lamps, and ice-box, but no toilet (a back balcony served for emergencies).

that perhaps St. Paul can return to its glory days as the center of the largest railway system in the world. Who knows—with Light Rail Transit and the push for high-speed trains in Minnesota, they might be right. In the meantime, curators at the Minnesota Transportation

Museum have settled for dreaming of someday connecting the round-house with the new downtown Science Museum by rail.

Jackson Street Roundhouse, 193 Pennsylvania Avenue East, (651) 228-0263 or 1-800-711-2591. From I-35E, take the Pennsylvania Avenue exit (no. 108) west to Jackson Street.

James J. Hill's millions made from his railroad empire gave him the clout to build on premier real estate across from the cathedral overlooking St. Paul.

St. Paul/Minneapolis

Schmidt and Grain Belt Breweries

A Tale of Two Beers

Minneapolis and St. Paul may be twins, but they're definitely not friends. St. Paul (Saint Small) is known as a big small town that's stuck in the past, whereas Minneapolis (Crimeapolis) has a superiority complex and compares itself to New York.

Historically, both towns vied to be the biggest in the state, and even kidnapped each other's census takers to try to sway the numbers. Legend says that St. Paul counted its dead for one of the censuses. Nothing highlights this rivalry more than the knock-down, drag-'em-out competition between Schmidt in St. Paul and Grain Belt in Minneapolis.

The early years focused more on keeping the beer industry alive than with fighting each other. One local brewery promoted its beer as "a family beverage and a perfect tonic promoting restful sleep and aiding appetite."

Declaring itself "pure food," Grain Belt was introduced in 1893. Advertisements said it was "Properly sterilized, Does not cause biliousness." Grain Belt was just what the doctor ordered, according to an ad from 1910:

> Quick Thought—Responsive Muscles. These qualities are dependent upon good health and athletes know the great value of GOOD BEER as a healthful builder of tissues wasted by exertion.

Hundreds of little breweries started up around the turn of the century, but most were eventually shut down due to Midwestern Puritanism. Anti-German sentiment around World War I only fueled the Prohibition movement, since beer was considered the drink of the German.

When Prohibition was repealed in 1933, Minnesota delayed signing on until the following year. In the meantime, the amount of alcohol allowed in "near beer" was raised from half a percent to 3.2 percent.

When the Minnesota Brewing Company bought the Schmidt brewery in 1991, they didn't buy the Schmidt brand. They held a contest to name its new beer, and "Pig's Eye" won hands down.

In 1891 the Minneapolis Brewing Company spent a half million dollars
to build the Grain Belt Brewery. Designed to be the largest, most high-tech
brewery in the world, it brewed 500,000 kegs annually. In the 1960s, an Old
World beer garden was constructed behind the garden, with a fountain and
tame deer for visitors to watch as they sipped beer.

High above Nicollet Island, the Grain Belt Beer Cap has loomed over the Mississippi since the 1940s. After lying dormant for fourteen years, the enormous sign next to the Hennepin Avenue Bridge was restored by G. Heileman Brewing Co. in 1989.

In spite of continued harassment from the temperance movement, Depression-era beer drinking skyrocketed. More people were drinking beer at home, because many of the bars were still shut down from Prohibition.

The battle of the beers heated up in the 1960s. Schmidt and Grain Belt signs hanging in bars would mysteriously disappear, only to be replaced by the competition. While on delivery runs, drivers would secretly vandalize the other brewer's kegs with motor oil, or tap them early to turn them to skunk beer.

Poley LaPage, a Schmidt salesman, was known for heavy-handed tactics and perhaps greasing the palms of a few bar owners to make

Schmidt the only beer served. He'd often stop by bars and buy a round of Schmidt for the regulars.

Grain Belt wasn't above underhanded practices either. When "The Syndicate" controlled by gangster Kid Cann was brought to federal court in St. Paul, Minneapolis Brewing Company (brewer of Grain Belt) was accused of having discounted beer sold to syndicate-controlled bars for thirty cents per case.

Another battleground was for the best brewing water. Schmidt touted its famous artesian water, but in 1963 the Minneapolis Brewing Company dug a new 1,074-foot well. "Perfect Brewing Water" soon appeared on cans of Grain Belt, along with views of their picturesque fountain and beer garden along the Mississippi. Schmidt simply stuck with "The Brew That Grew with the Great Northwest."

While the third big brewery in town, Hamm's, had a cuddly and clumsy bear as its mascot, Minneapolis Brewing Company introduced "The Grain Belt Guys," who tried to lure their buddies out of uncomfortable situations. One ad featured the guys wiggling bottles of Grain Belt at a groom as his bride walks down the aisle. Ironically, the teetotalers during Prohibition warned against exactly this—husbands abandoning their families for the bar. The ad was pulled after the United Presbyterian Church formally protested.

Meanwhile, clouds were darkening downriver. Having been sold to G. Heileman in 1972, Schmidt's claim of "Honest to Minnesota" seemed farfetched. "Minnesotans who were loyal to Schmidt as one of the last real hometown brews now began to boycott it along with other Heileman brands," according to Jeff Lonto in *Legend of the Brewery: A Brief History of the Minneapolis Brewing Heritage.*

Grain Belt's problems came to a head after Irwin Jacobs bought the brewery at the beginning of 1975 and ran it into the ground. The last beer was shipped out on Christmas Day 1975. Grain Belt, as well, was sold to G. Heileman.

In 1976, an auction was held, and every last bit of brewing equipment was sold off. Jacobs tried to bulldoze the brewery numerous times, but the people of Northeast Minneapolis halted him. The building is now being renovated into office space for RSP Architects.

Heileman also decided to close the Schmidt brewery and sell off the old equipment. Luckily, the Minnesota Brewing Company bought it in 1991 and kept all the employees working.

Since the Minnesota Brewing Company didn't own the Schmidt

name, its most successful beer was named after St. Paul founder and notorious scoundrel "Pig's Eye" Parrant. Ironically, Grain Belt is now brewed in St. Paul as well, since the Minnesota Brewing Company bought that name from Heileman.

Grain Belt Brew House, 1220 Marshall Street NE. From I-94, take the Broadway Street exit and go east across the Mississippi River. The brewery is visible from the bridge on the left.

Schmidt/Landmark Brewery, Minnesota Brewing Company, 882 West Seventh Street, (651) 228-9173. From I-94 eastbound, take the Fifth Street exit to West Seventh Street (Highway 5). Turn right and follow it for almost a mile. Look for the big bottle of beer on your left and the brewery behind it.

Sauk Centre

Sinclair Lewis's Hometown

Main Street, U.S.A.

When Sinclair Lewis revealed the petty gossip of small-town life in his novel *Main Street*, the residents of Sauk Centre were not amused. He thinly veiled his satire by naming the town "Gopher Prairie," but the nickname, combining Minnesota's state rodent and the terrain of his hometown, couldn't conceal his intended target. Locals often recognized themselves as characters in compromising situations. Lewis wasn't concerned with being endeared to his peers; perhaps he held a grudge after being fired from his job as a clerk at the Palmer House Hotel for reading books and daydreaming when he should have been working.

Lewis kept up his biting wit in *Babbitt* and *Elmer Gantry*, eventually completing twenty-three novels. When he was awarded the Pulitzer Prize for literature in 1926 for *Arrowsmith,* he simply refused it. Even becoming the first American to win the Nobel Prize for literature in 1930 didn't change his perspective.

Lewis had become a national treasure, and his second wife, Dorothy Thompson Lewis, was a well-known journalist. She was the first woman to head the foreign office of a major American newspaper, and her column "On the Record" was syndicated in more than two hundred newspapers.

For a while, Lewis lived in St. Paul, down the street from F. Scott Fitzgerald's rowhouse on Summit Avenue. Lewis appreciated the city life of St. Paul and the majestic houses, but Fitzgerald often complained that his hometown was too provincial. Chances are the two writers never met, but perhaps they could have exchanged notes about their towns and the greener pastures over the fence.

Sauk Centre forgave its ungrateful son and how: "Original Main Street" is now posted on the street signs; the park has been renamed "Sinclair Lewis City Park"; and even the high school football team is named the "Mainstreeters."

The annual town festival in mid-July celebrates Sinclair Lewis Days with a Ms. Sauk Centre pageant and milk-carton boat races. Off I-94, the Sinclair Lewis Museum and Interpretive Center displays old manuscripts and charts the writer's life.

Sinclair Lewis's boyhood home on Sinclair Lewis Avenue, just three blocks from Main Street, has been placed on the National Register of Historic Places and can be visited daily from Memorial Day through Labor Day.

The Palmer House Hotel, built in 1901, ranks as one of the more interesting sites in Sauk Centre to get a feel for Lewis's era, since it provided a backdrop for both *Work of Art* and *Main Street*. Whether you spend the night or just stop in for tea, browse through the historical photos scattered on the walls and imagine the disgruntled worker as the struggling writer in the making.

Sinclair Lewis Museum and Interpretive Center, (320) 352-5201. Located at the juncture of I-94 and Highway 71.

Sinclair Lewis's Boyhood Home, 810 Sinclair Lewis Avenue. Summer only; winter by appointment.

The Palmer House Hotel, 228 Main Street at Sinclair Lewis Avenue, (320) 352-3431.

Sauk Rapids

Molehill Rock Garden

Reincarnation Paradise

" **A** crazy man is a lazy man; a lazy man is a crazy man. That is why a lazy man is crazy in getting money so he can remain lazy," according to the pamphlet *The Heart of Theosophy.* Louis Wippich, the author, definitely wasn't lazy—at least in this life.

In 1932, Wippich dreamed of creating "the largest, most beautiful rock garden in America" out of slabs of red stone from the area. His job as a mechanic gave him access to all kinds of old metal objects to add to his "Molehill Rock Garden" behind his house.

When the Security Federal Bank in St. Cloud was ripped down, Wippich saw a gold mine of granite. "He hired every kid in town," remembers neighbor Jim Roberts. "In those days you could hire 'em for twenty cents a day." All the urchins in the neighborhood hauled slabs of stone to erect a forty-five-foot tower and a mini-version of the Parthenon in Athens. Wippich set aside some of the granite from the bank to build his house. He ended up renting out his home and living in the garage to earn money to expand his garden.

"Different school buses would come from all over the state to visit Louis's Rock Garden," according to Roberts. "He'd say, 'I did it myself with my one hundred boys!'" In leading little tours around his rock garden, Wippich would jokingly throw in a few of his strangely profound wordplays, à la Dr. Seuss, based on his spiritualist Theosophy to amuse the children.

Timeless Time

Time never began; people only began to time it off. But it did not affect the timeless time anyhow. So don't forget the pathway to timeless time as it still is. And it is time to time out of time and go into timeless time golessly [sic]. So time yourself out of time; even take time to do that timely act in time (meditate), time your meditating

Louis Wippich built Molehill as a garden to return to in his next life.

time on time (same hour), then you, the timer, will time smoothly along on the timed path, (like your car-timer on the highway), onto the heart of timeless time (timeless time is the same as duration, no feeling of chopped up in small pieces. Time not timed off, is infinite, pieceless).

He compiled a number of these cryptic visions in a 1948 pamphlet published in "Sauk Rapids, Minnesota, the home of the portable office of the Vision Sublime." According to the booklet, "the home office of our home universe for this planet—earth" is Tibet, which makes sense considering Wippich's many references to Buddhist philosophy.

His New Age vision even included hatha yoga, but at the time neighbors simply considered him bizarre yet fun. Wippich wrote that humor is the ultimate salvation and warned against becoming too intellectual. "Don't be too anxious to get smart because when you get smart everything appears foolish. . . . And on top of that, lots of dizzy people will ask you carloads of dizzy questions to answer."

The question of why Louis built the rock garden remains a mystery. His neighbors Jim and Joyce Roberts maintain that "he thought he'd be reincarnated as a bird; this was going to be his playground. . . . A few weeks after his brother Gus died, he came to a friend of his and said, 'Gus is back.' 'How did you know?' his friend asked. 'I saw his eyes. He came back as a salamander.'"

The nickname "Molehill" probably stems from the "Sermon on Mole Hill" in his booklet. The garden is a sort of launching pad into the next world, as "your solid mole hill to stand on for your intellectual feet to advance one more step in the changing modern world ladder."

Louis's rock garden was completed after twenty-six years of hard labor, mostly by neighborhood youngsters, in 1958 (or the year 56 in the Age of Aquarius). Wippich died in 1973, and his rock garden is not inundated with school tours anymore. Little information remains about Molehill, except for a short documentary called "St. Cloud Sleep."

Three young women at the local Dairy Queen giggle that they heard he buried his wife there and the whole garden is an elaborate monument to her. They add that teenagers sneak in there at night to make out in the romantic and scary setting.

Another rumor (which actually could be true) is that Wippich used to sit around stark naked in his garden, perhaps waiting for aliens. Among occasional references in his manual to UFOs, he writes about the "FOURTH DIMENSION: Undress me to be clean, nude among the nudeless is all I ask. . . . Who can stand nude among the nudeless? Yanky Doodles (???) Noodles for you, you nude head!!!"

Jim and Joyce Roberts remember Wippich as a character. They even hint that maybe he knew something we don't. Sitting in their backyard, they note, "Everytime we see blackbirds up there [in the garden] we say, 'That's Gus and that's Louis.'" Then they laugh, "Well, I guess it can't be Gus, since he's a salamander."

Molehill Rock Garden, corner of Third Avenue North and Sixth Street (private residence). From Highway 10, turn off the highway toward Sauk Rapids. Before getting to downtown, turn left up the hill on Sixth Street. Drive a few blocks and look for the granite tower on the left.

Soudan

Soudan Mine

Journey to the Center of the Earth

Put on that hard hat, wrap your coat around tightly, and prepare to enter the earth. The Tower-Soudan tour is the only underground mine tour in the United States, and perfect for scorching hot summer days since the temperature is a mere 50° in the tunnels.

No need to hum "Canary in a Coal Mine" since the Vermillion Range is known as "The Cadillac of Mines." No poisonous gas has ever been detected and the hard rock is perfect for tunneling (only thirteen men have ever died in it!).

The tour begins with an eight-minute video extolling the virtues of mining. Visitors then adjust the size of their hard hats and get ready to go underground.

The covered cage/elevator descends straight down at a mere ten miles per hour, but it feels like it's falling. Within three minutes, the tour is 2,341 feet into the earth in the oldest mine in the state. "This is the closest to China many of you folks will ever be," Andy the guide points out.

As the tour group piles onto an underground train, one of the tourists asks, "Haven't lots of people died from working in the mines?"

Andy, who is obviously used to skeptics, replies assuredly, "Mining is dangerous work, but the Tower-Soudan mine is the safest in the state."

"Considering we're 689 feet below sea level, don't you worry about the mine shaft filling up with water?" continues the questioner.

"That's why we have pumps to prevent a flood," Andy answers.

The tourist seems almost disappointed that the mine isn't more dangerous and asks, "But don't people get sick from the lack of light?"

"Not more than being in a cubicle in a skyscraper forty stories in the air!" Andy retorts. Before motorized train cars, mules would pull the ore and they would stay underground for half a year without ever coming up. Since only candles were used in the shafts, the poor beasts' eyes were covered when they were brought to the surface. The bandages were removed slowly to allow light in, so they wouldn't go blind.

Andy breaks into song to try to calm the troubled tourists:

> My sweetheart's a mule in the mine.
> I can drive her without any lines.
> On the ore car I sit,
> I chew snoose and I spit
> all over my sweetheart's behind.

Laughs echo in the mine shaft and the group jams into the three-level elevator to rise to the surface. While the lift is bouncing back and forth, the doubting tourist tries one last time, almost pleading, "Have you ever had a major catastrophe?"

Secure that hard hat and prepare to descend into the center of the earth. Here is the mine's lower level one year after it closed operations.

"Never," the guide replies, not missing a beat. "That's why it's called 'The Cadillac of Mines'!"

Tower-Soudan Mine, (218) 753-2245 or 1-800-766-6000. Drive northeast of Tower on Highway 169. Look for signs for the mine just north of Soudan. Summer only.

Sparta, Wisconsin

F.A.S.T.

Where the Statues Come From

" **L**ook! A giant cheeseburger!" exclaims Jerry Vettrus as he shows visitors around "the graveyard," a field of enormous fiberglass figures and molds for everything from giant cows to King Kong in Sparta, Wisconsin. As we pass a couple of Big Boys, he says, "A guy called me asking for a couple of Big Boys for his yard. He didn't want them painted, he just wanted to look at them."

F.A.S.T. (Fiberglass Animals, Shapes, and Trademarks) is a factory of roadside Americana. Its roots stretch back to a small company called Sculptured Advertising from Minneapolis, which went out of business in 1974. The phoenix rising from its ashes was called Creative Displays, and then finally F.A.S.T. in 1983. Jerry Vettrus just bought out his F.A.S.T. partner, Norb Anderson: "As part of the agreement, I have to make him a thirteen-foot dairy cow."

Many of F.A.S.T.'s fiberglass behemoths once inhabited a mini-putt golf course run by Norb Anderson next to the Minnesota State Fairgrounds on Como Avenue. Alas! No more putting through the legs of enormous moose and cows; the State Fair needed a larger parking lot.

Creative Displays/F.A.S.T.'s most original work was in their early years: the 45-foot Jolly Green Giant in Blue Earth and the breathtaking 145-foot, walk-through muskie in Hayward, Wisconsin. Now F.A.S.T. statues are headed all over the world—slides to Cyprus, dog fountains to Brazil, and an aquasplash to Italy—but most of their business still comes from the Wisconsin Dells and small-town Minnesota.

Moira Harris, in her book *Monumental Minnesota*, writes that in 1990, "Guidelines for 'Celebrate Minnesota' had suggested that towns seek ways to celebrate their history and welcome former residents home." Many Minnesota towns decided the best way to celebrate their heritage was to erect an enormous animal sculpture. Nothing lures tourists off the interstate like a huge fiberglass fish.

An uncooked Big Boy in the F.A.S.T. fiberglass graveyard.

Vettrus's technique requires "a fiberglass gun and lots of foam to make the mold. It takes a thousand dollars' worth of foam to make a twenty-two-foot high pirate," he states matter-of-factly. "I've already sent three pirates to Hong Kong, but they wanted one even bigger." Apparently, buying bulk statues pays off. "The first A&W Bear I made cost twelve thousand dollars. Since I then had the mold, the second one was only eight thousand!"

F.A.S.T. has a five-page price list of already-made molds ready to form a sculpture costing anywhere from seven hundred dollars and up. Hmmm, won't the Joneses turn green after we place a fourteen-foot Spartan on our suburban plot?

Vettrus prefers designing original sculptures. "Appleton needed a heart slide," he says, "but it had to be anatomically correct. We consulted with a doctor, and now children can climb right through the aorta!"

Even though their huge fiberglass sculptures scream out to be noticed, F.A.S.T. is a relatively well-kept secret. Jerry Vettrus doesn't mind, though, and keeps a zen-like attitude. "People fifty miles from here don't even know we exist! But that's OK, because we know we exist."

Creative Display/F.A.S.T. Selected Credits:

- Chief Red Robe in Thief River Falls, 1976
- Voyageur in Cloquet, 1976
- Serpent in Crosby, 1977
- Jolly Green Giant in Blue Earth, 1978
- Leaping Stag in Deerwood, 1978
- Chief Wenonga in Battle Lake, 1979
- Ojibwe and Sioux statues, Thunderbird Hotel, Bloomington, 1970s
- Iron Worker in Aitkin, 1981
- Robin Hood north of Garrison, 1982
- Eagle in Remer, 1983
- Bear in Hill City, 1985
- Blackduck's black duck, 1985
- Hobo in Starbuck, 1987
- Trout in Preston, 1988

- Moose in Moose Lake, 1989
- Chicken in Delano, 1990
- Crow in Belgrade, 1990
- Elephant spout, Amusement City, St. Paul, 1999

F.A.S.T., (608) 269-7110. Once in Sparta, Wisconsin, look for the World's Largest Bicyclist, then turn north on Highway 21 for about three miles. Look for the hamburger and buffalo sculptures. No organized tours.

Stillwater

Vittorio's Bootlegger Caves

Spelunking in Style

Jules St. Pierre ventured into the Stillwater area with his Native American wife in 1836. He noticed fresh spring water bubbling to the surface and began digging a cave into the limestone hill to protect the goods he traded with the tribes.

Although the French continued carving away at the cliff for years, not until 1848 did anyone realize the perfect use for these caves: beer. The Empire Brewery took advantage of the constant source of water plus the constant 52° of the caves to brew and store huge hogsheads.

Although the tunnel expansion was halted during the Civil War, the shoveling continued, and a new brewery was opened in the 1880s. The Joseph Wolf Brewery and the attached Pacific Hotel were the hottest spots north of Chicago for the next fifty years.

During Prohibition, brewing continued as usual, but the secret entrance was in back of the blacksmith's shop next door. You had to knock twice for the saloon, three times for the second-story dance hall, and show your money to enter the third-floor bordello, or "house of ill-repute," according to a brochure on the building.

Al Capone used to run liquor out the back, and wanted to keep expanding the caves with shovels or dynamite to store more hooch. The Feds got wise when an explosion inside blew up a section of the cave and wine leaked out the opening. The Minnesota Highway Department—perhaps on a tip from Elliot Ness—closed the caves in the 1930s.

Tom "The Cave Man" Curtis bought the caves in 1945 and spent the next years digging and leading tours. He told tales of King Neptune living deep in the tunnel with his legions of leprechauns. Kids would stare into "the bottomless pit," which he claimed went all the way to China. "I've thought about hanging a dummy upside down . . . he'd be rightside up according to the reflection," he said.

A shaft in the cave that was used as a well can be seen rising all the

Dug by hand in the 1840s, Vittorio's Caves at the entrance to Stillwater have been used for everything from bomb shelters to tunnels of love. Now they have been returned to one of their original purposes—storing beer.

way to the top of the hill, which is now a parking lot. Curtis's explanation was that it was used for smoke signals when the Sioux fought with the Ojibwe, with puffs visible for miles along the St. Croix Valley.

Curtis hooked up an elaborate system of cables on the ground, then flooded the caves with just enough water so flatbed wooden boats could be pulled through. "Kinda like a tunnel of love," says a tour guide. Although the water has now been drained, one of the original boats is still on display.

The Cave Man seduced tourists with a wishing well, sportsmen with a fishing hole (fed with trout), and townspeople with a bomb shelter in the 1950s. Schoolchildren were brought to practice their civil defense drills. Curtis equipped the caves with emergency rations and advertised them as the safest place in town: "If it hadn't cost so much overtime, I'd have hired a couple of Russian pilots to drop a few test bombs to prove my point."

The next owner of the complex was Vittorio Gozzi from Bologna, Italy, who married a Swede named Sondra and decided to settle in Stillwater. Inspired by the enchanting island of Capri near Naples, Vittorio transformed a cave that was being used to repair cars into the amazing Grotto Blue Dining Room. The roof of the cavern is flooded in cobalt blue light and the walls are painted with picturesque Mediterranean islands. According to *Star Tribune* food critic Jeremy Iggers, the waiters are "like extras from *The Godfather*." The Grotto Blue is a favorite for prom dates, with its elegant urns and busts of Roman legionnaires as if they're in the catacombs under the Colosseum awaiting Caesar's lions! This romantic relic from 1969 is still one of the swankiest hot spots in town.

Upstairs from the Grotto Blue is what was once the Pacific Hotel, which Lynn Most, the owner, wants to turn back into an inn like the old days. Secret passages built into the cliff that haven't been opened since Prohibition are still being uncovered. Recently when the walls were being redone, a huge room that could easily seat two hundred people was discovered from Stillwater's speakeasy days. According to Most, "We think there's one they haven't found yet that seats a hundred people."

As of 1998, the Joseph Wolf Brewery is brewing again. More than 25,000 barrels a year flow of Hazel Wolf's Nut Brown Ale, Porter, Imperial Stout, Pils, and German Wheat, but only Vittorio's has them on tap.

Tours of the limestone caves still run every summer, and guides are proud to point out every historical detail about the caves, including the fact that Bing Crosby's mother, Kate Harrigan, was born next to the caves and grew up in Stillwater.

The largest section of the cave is "the reception room," where a few wedding parties are held every year amidst the handmade barrels and the old straw-covered Chianti bottles strewn about for ragtime atmosphere.

Excavation continues into the hillside. According to the guides, "Vittorio's attempted to connect with the original Joseph Wolf Brewery, but it took two men two full weeks with the help of electrical jackhammers to progress fifteen feet!"

Although the haunted cave tours ended a few years ago, the guides throw in the tale of the three spelunkers from the University of Minnesota who were lost in the "boomsite" cave just north of Stillwater in the 1960s. One of the group was buried alive, and his cries can still be heard coming out of that cave. That's when the guide turns the light out so you can experience the complete darkness.

Vittorio's Restaurant and Caves, 402 South Main Street, (651) 439-3588 or (651) 439-3538. From the Twin Cities, take Highway 36 east to Stillwater. The caves are on the left, just before downtown. Caves open summer only.

While in the Area

Locals may lament the changes of the past fifteen years, but the "Jewel of the St. Croix" still has one of the best assortments of Victorian-era houses in the state. Downtown has been overrun with antique stores, but they also serve as a stretch of little museums.

The official town museum, the Washington County Historical Society, is set in an old 1850s building on the site where a duel to the death was supposedly fought between a Dakota and an Ojibwe chief. Stillwater calls itself "The Birthplace of Minnesota" since a group of settlers in town declared Minnesota a territory and sent Henry Hastings Sibley to the U.S. Congress to make it official. Photos document the old Stillwater logging days and the building of the state penitentiary.

Washington County Historical Society, 602 North Main Street, (651) 439-5956.

For down-home American food with hearty meatloaf specials and occasional Sam Shepard sightings, stop in the Main Cafe, obviously on Main Street.

Brine's Bar and Restaurant (219 South Main Street, [651] 439-1862) used to be a sideline to the delicatessen downstairs, but the deli from 1958 is now gone. For malts and roast beef sandwiches the restaurant can't be beat.

While the Lowell Inn (102 North Second Street, [651] 439-1100) is a tad pricey, anyplace that calls itself "The Mount Vernon of the West," with waitresses dressed in different colonial themes, deserves some respect.

The Minnesota Zephyr train from the 1940s puffs through the St. Croix Valley, serving a hearty dinner of game birds, flounder, or steak. The three-hour tour is rounded out with a performance by the Zephyr Cabaret. 601 North Main, (651) 430-3000 or 1-800-992-6100.

Two Harbors

3M/Dwan Sandpaper Museum
Keeping the World Smooth

If they would have used the correct kind of sandpaper on the Hubble telescope, it wouldn't have malfunctioned, costing taxpayers billions of dollars. Sounds impossible, but that is just one of the many facts to be learned from the display of different grades of sandpaper in the 3M/ Dwan Museum.

Speculation rages about whether NASA could have saved us all a pile of money on the heat-sensitive tiles that kept falling off the space shuttle if they would have just given the Sandpaper Museum a ring for advice on the right grade paper.

Located in the 1902 house of John Dwan (one of the four founders of 3M), the museum has demonstrations of how Dwan and his cohorts smeared glue on paper, magnetically charged it, and then dropped bits of Lake Superior sand on it. With this simple technique, 3M went from a little adhesive producer to a multinational giant.

More breakthroughs were around the corner, such as wet or dry sandpaper for different levels of abrasion. Scotch tape was introduced in 1928. Magnetic recording tape soon followed, along with cellophane and other kinds of sticky tape. The most recent revelation, Post-It Notes, were designed by fluke in the lab.

In spite of these innovations, it all began with sandpaper. After showing how different grades of paper are used, the museum generously hands out free samples to try at home. Maybe a NASA representative will finally take a tour and use the right sandpaper!

According to curator Jeff McMorrow, quoted in *America's Strangest Museums,* "They may be skeptical at first, but by the time they're done, they've learned a lot and have a new appreciation of sandpaper."

3M/Dwan Sandpaper Museum, 201 Waterfront Drive, (218) 834-4898. Take Highway 61 into Two Harbors and turn right on Waterfront Drive.

The museum is on the right side of the road before downtown. Check with the Lake County Historical Society a block farther down for tours.

While in the Area

Be sure and stop for a photo by the roadside landmark, Pierre the Voyageur, standing next to the Voyageur Hotel. He's now in a popularity contest with the hunting and fishing store behind him, which boasts a real jackalope. Made of two telephone poles covered by a ton of stucco, the twenty-foot-tall Pierre used to sport movable eyes that would gyrate back and forth as tourists passed on Highway 61.

A bright red fiberglass rooster reaching twelve feet into the air greets visitors coming to Two Harbors from the south. One year, the

With his head in the clouds, Pierre continues to mark the spot of the Voyageur Hotel in Two Harbors on Highway 61. Built from a pair of telephone poles, the French-Canadian monument used to have eyes that would swing back and forth as traffic zipped by.

This striking red-and-white, twelve-foot rooster greets the morning and all the visitors entering Two Harbors, hoping they'll stop and browse at the gift shop behind it.

graduating class at the high school stole the rooster as a prank, and headlines in a local paper supposedly read "12 Foot Cock Stolen." When asked about their chicken, the clerks in the gift shop are strangely silent and just say that they wanted something to draw tourists.

The North Shore is famous for pies and smoked fish. The old standby for Lake Superior whitefish, turkey jerky, and smoked cheese is Lou's Fish on the north side of town on Highway 61. They even have a website: Lousfish.com.

Better arrive early at Betty's Pies, just a few miles east of Two Harbors on Highway 61, if you want to get your pick of pastry. After a chicken pasty and a slice or two of homemade blueberry pie, step out the door and take a walk on the Stewart River to burn off those calories.

Vining

Small Town Sculpture Park

Home of the Swollen Big Toe

"**D**ifferent, isn't it?" says Ken Nyberg about his Big Foot statue, which has what looks like a painfully distended toe. His explanation for the sculpture? "Can't really go wrong with a foot since there's billions of them, and they're all different."

Nyberg's foot, made out of ten-gauge steel, stands at the entrance to the tiny town of Vining along Highway 210. The owner of the Citgo Station at the edge of town was so inspired by the sculpture that he renamed his store "The Big Foot Gas Station."

Everyone has a different theory on the meaning of the foot. "A doctor wrote me a letter calling it a 'Hawaiian hitchhiker's toe,'" Nyberg laughs. His only attempt at an explanation is, "I didn't want to do anything with a person in it." He says he even thought of doing a statue of a big middle finger once, "But I don't think many people would like that."

Art critics could easily parallel his work to Claes Oldenburg, whose spoon and cherry bridge is the prize of the Walker Sculpture Garden, and whose clothespin has become the symbol of downtown Philadelphia. In fact, Nyberg welded a huge clothespin as well (a different design), which is standing in the center of Vining.

Nyberg spent ten years as a construction worker, but now works part time and makes colossal sculptures on the weekend and during the winter. He collects scrap steel from his job, then welds the pieces together in an unusual patchwork pattern. The enormous sculptures are all around Vining and outside his Quonset hut workshop on the edge of town. Nyberg is unassuming about them, saying that he just makes them for fun. When asked what the titles of the sculptures are, he replies, "Oh, you can call them whatever you want."

He doesn't seem to mind that his work is open to interpretation. A huge pair of silver pliers ready to crush a large insect is fixed outside the Big Foot Gas Station. "Some people think it's a beetle, a cricket, or

Ken Nyberg remains cryptic about the muse that inspired this foot with the painfully swollen big toe. He leaves it open to interpretation, commenting only, "I didn't want to do anything with a person in it."

even a woodtick," Nyberg says, preferring to let people construe his work any way they want.

Little by little, his sculptures are becoming well known around the area. Ottertail City commissioned him to construct a giant otter with a fish in its paw as the new town symbol. The local Lion's Club also

At the Big Foot Gas Station and Sculpture Garden, a coffee cup pours out its insides and is held up by the stream of java; enormous tubes of steel form an iron square knot; and a shiny pliers is ready to squash an unsuspecting bug. "Some people think it's a beetle, a cricket, or even a woodtick," says Nyberg, careful not to give away its true identity.

convinced Nyberg to weld a (what else?) giant lion that is carried around to local parades on a trailer.

When asked if he's going to do a Paul Bunyan statue, Nyberg responds, "No, I want to do something else," then adds with a twinkle in his eye, "I think there are already enough Paul Bunyans around."

Ken Nyberg's sculptures. Vining is about twenty-five miles east of I-94 and Fergus Falls on Highway 210.

Virginia

World's Largest Floating Loon

Decoy on Silver Lake

The loon's haunting cries on the more than 10,000 lakes in Minnesota have instigated a rush of towns claiming the bird as their own. Even our northern neighbors, the Canadians, tried to appropriate the red-eyed diver, stamping the bird's image on their one-dollar coin, the "loony."

The loon is Minnesota's state bird, and we've got the statues to prove it! Both International Falls and the Bemidji fairgrounds have loon sculptures, but the most remarkable winged behemoth floats proudly on Silver Lake in Virginia. Hearing about Virginia's loon, Mercer, Wisconsin, decided to up the ante with their sixteen-foot "Claire de Loon," which can talk to tourists. About the same time as this rivalry was heating up, Virginia's bird took a mysterious beating during a thunderstorm and nearly sank.

The Minnesota town gallantly refrained from resorting to the usual epithets against our cheese-eating neighbors and simply beefed up their loon to top Wisconsin's alleged World's Largest Loon. Now Virginia's twenty-foot-long, ten-foot-high loon, built by Bill Martin in 1982, is dutifully hauled into the shed each winter to keep the town symbol from sinking (and safe from cross-border hoodlums). What could be the World's Largest Decoy is the centerpiece for Virginia's annual Land of the Loon Festival in June.

Other northern towns celebrate Minnesota's twelve thousand loons by staging loon-calling contests. Loon Fest in Brainerd goes head-to-head with Mosquito Fest at the beginning of July. Nisswa, which holds the claim of "Loon Capital of the World," is home to the North American Loon-Calling Competition—in between their famous turtle races. Call (218) 454-1400 for information about Nisswa's loon contest, or (218) 963-2620 or 1-800-950-9610 to rent a racing turtle. Snapping turtles prohibited.

Molded out of concrete in 1963, the loon in Vergas stands twenty feet tall. "Just drive around Loon Lake," the waitress at the Loon Café says. "It's huge—you can't miss it!"

Silver Lake in downtown Virginia used to boast a famous monkey house on the shore, as well as its very own Virginia beer, Iron Brew. Now it features a huge floating loon bouncing on the waves, which serves as the centerpiece for the annual Loon Festival.

Wabasha

Anderson House Hotel
Working Sleeper Cats

U pon opening the door to the hotel room, a little "Mreow" ema-
nates from the crack. Ah, home at last—or at least that's the de-
sired effect. A large cat is just waiting to be loved with his own litter
box, cat bowl, and little instruction manual:

> Hello! My name is Spook. Thank you for selecting me, I promise
> you won't be sorry. I was born here at the Anderson House. Thanks
> to all the attention I received from the staff as a kitten I am the most
> lovable cat in town. I will kiss you and hug you whenever I can. I
> love to be held and loved and I will talk to you at will. I also love to
> be around small children.

Working dogs, sure, but working cats? The Anderson House from
1856, the oldest running hotel in Minnesota (and west of the Mississippi, for that matter), provides specially trained "sleeper cats" to comfort road-weary travelers and warm their hand-sewn quilts. If that's
not enough, hot bricks covered with a quilted envelope can heat up the
antique beds, and even old-fashioned mustard plasters can be requested
to cure a cold.

The life of a "sleeper cat" can be perilous, though. Once the favorite of all fifteen cats in the hotel, Morris, was nearly kidnapped by
a college kid. "The potential abductor tried to take Morris down the
backstairs, but he yowled, and one of the employees heard it and came
out and rescued him. We told that college boy it was just as well he
didn't come back," fourth-generation owner John Hall told the *Washington Post.*

In general, the cats live long, healthy lives, and only one accident
has happened since the cats have been put to work. A little Himalayan
named Muffie was adopted by a couple "whose little boy was hyper-
active. They checked out early in the morning and left the cat awaiting

The favorite kitty of Anderson House, Spook the Sleeper Cat, has a busy schedule, working nights to keep guests toasty and content.

a visit to our vet," according to Hall. Rumor has it the cat ran out of lives.

The hotel's atmosphere is homey without being too "precious," as some B & Bs can be. Sure there's the cookie jar in the lobby and antique furniture in every room, but a visit to the catroom shows that the Anderson House is unique. All the cats have their own sleeping box with their name over it as they rest up for the night shift. Our cat, for example, was so well rested that at 3:00 A.M. he did laps around the room—all twenty pounds of him. Maybe that's why he's called Spook.

The Anderson House restaurant is famous for old-world specialties, such as enormous Dutch cinnamon rolls, Dutch oven steaks, ham pot-pie, apple brandy pie, and baked raisin beans. Guests who fish can ask the kitchen to fry up their catch for supper. Their Pennsylvania Dutch recipes have been gathered in the *Anderson House Cookbook*.

Anderson House Hotel, 333 West Main Street, (651) 565-4525 or 1-800-535-5467. Wabasha is ninety minutes south of the Twin Cities on Highway 61. Take the Wabasha exit east toward the Mississippi. Turn left on Main Street, go under a bridge, and the hotel is on the left.

While in the Area

Cries of "The steamboat is coming! The steamboat is coming!" and news of the impending arrival of the *Delta Queen,* the *American Queen,* or the *Mississippi Queen* are the talk of the town in the summer. In the winter, residents may be proud of the Grumpy Old Men Festival, with ice-shack contests inspired by the movie, but the real excitement is eight hundred bald eagles wintering nearby. At press time, the Great American Bald Eagle Interpretive Center was in the process of being built.

Walnut Grove

Laura Ingalls Wilder Tour
Little Museum on the Prairie

O f all the towns that maintain the title of the original "Little House on the Prairie," perhaps Walnut Grove has the best claim. Laura Ingalls Wilder wrote about her family's experience in *On the Banks of Plum Creek,* set in 1873 but not published until 1937.

After moving out of the house in the big woods, Pa and the gang homesteaded in Redwood County. With few trees in the area, the family set to work building a "dugout," a sod house partially shoveled into a hillside to reduce the number of grass bricks needed to be cut from the thick and stubborn sod. The Ingallses' dugout site, off County Road 5, can be visited, but only in the summer, since it's on Harold Gordon's private farm.

Next stop is off the Laura Ingalls Wilder Highway, near Walnut Grove, where a small museum displays the Wilder Bible, a homemade quilt, and historical photos. The neighbor's house, the Nelsons', is even on the site. In a twist of representation versus reality, Pa's gun and powderhorn (actually, Michael Landon's) are exhibited for fans of the *Little House on the Prairie* TV show.

In July, the town comes out in force for the annual Laura Ingalls Wilder parade, and high-tech sets and special effects complete the old-fashioned "Fragments of a Dream" pageant, reenacting scenes from *Little House on the Prairie* books.

Although the Ingallses' soddy home protected them from the cold winters and the summer grass fires, swarms of grasshoppers two years in a row forced the famous pioneer family to abandon their sod house on the banks of Plum Creek.

Laura Ingalls Wilder Museum, (507) 859-2155 or (507) 859-2358. From Walnut Grove, go east on Highway 14 about eight miles to County Road 5. Turn right and follow the signs to the museum.

While in the Area

To top off the Little House on the Prairie experience, spend a night like the pioneers in an 1880 replica sod house twenty miles east of Walnut Grove. To make the walls solid enough for the soddy, Stan McCone had to find virgin prairie—a rarity in Minnesota and usually protected land. Luckily, a buddy on the next farm had a little patch, and McCone fought the same battle as the early settlers to chop through the thick prairie sod.

With 150 tons of grass bricks piled high, the cozy one-room sod house was finished. "This is my husband's 'field of dreams,'" says his wife, Virginia, to tourists as they wander around the ten acres of restored prairie. Stan stacked sod for two houses, a "Poorman's Dugout," with the roof made of cottonwood poles topped with grass, and the "Rich Man's Soddy," where guests stay.

The Wilders probably lived in a house like the first one, whereas guests at the B & B shack up in the second. In pioneer days, lumber was too expensive for most people and tar paper for the ceiling was considered a luxury item. However, a downpour would ruin the pioneer experience if the McCones hadn't weatherproofed the house.

A night at this prairie B & B comes complete with oil lamps, a wood-burning stove, and vintage clothes to enhance the experience.

McCones' sod house, 12598 Magnolia Avenue, (507) 723-5138. From Walnut Grove, take Highway 14 east just past Highway 71 and look for signs.

Sleeping in a sod house may not be the lap of luxury, but Laura Ingalls Wilder wasn't spoiled with running water, wooden floors, and a leakproof roof like the guests at this B & B are.

Winona

Julius C. Wilkie Steamboat

Steam Breaks Speed Records

Ever since the steamboat *Virginia* ventured north on the Mississippi in 1823, the area that would become Minnesota has never been the same. Steam engines replaced flatbedded keelboats, fifty to eighty feet long, which used sails or oars planted into the shoreline and walked to the back of the boat. Even with side- or stern-wheel steamboats, however, the journey from St. Louis to Fort Snelling took twenty days.

By the 1840s, it became fashionable to cruise up the river by steamboat to see the land purchased from France and the new west's teepee villages. First-class trips stopped at all the river towns along the way, including Winona, so tourists could visit this wild frontier.

The public was awestruck when the speedy *Grey Eagle* steamboat zoomed up the river at 13 miles per hour for twenty-four hours and forty minutes, covering 265 miles and setting a new world record. In 1870, a duel was declared between the *Natchez* and the *Robert E. Lee* steamboats when both declared themselves the fastest steamboat in the world. A huge oil painting of "The Great Mississippi River Race of 1870" between New Orleans and St. Louis hangs in the Winona museum.

Speed wasn't the only rage, as historical photos in the museum show. The Sprague claimed the title of the largest stern-wheel towboat in the world, measuring 276 feet by 61 feet; it set the all-time world record by pulling 67,000 tons of coal up the Mississippi. The behemoth lasted until 1948, when owners disposed of it with a match.

Most of these huge boats only lasted around five years because of inevitable damage to the hull due to the unpredictability of the Mississippi River bottom. Then the wooden steamboats were either dragged to the side of the river to rot or torched to keep the riverway clear.

Winona's *Julius C. Wilkie* steamboat avoided the flames until 1981, when it was "accidentally" burned down. Fire officials said the blaze "needed some help" since there were no electrical fixtures or heaters around to start it. The steamboat has now been restored as a museum and is permanently docked at Levee Park. Visitors can see blueprints of the boats, freight bills dating back to 1864, old engines, and new videos depicting steam's glory days. But just as flatbedded keelboats replaced voyageur canoes, "The Golden Age of Steamboats" gave way to "The Golden Age of Railroads" around 1880.

Julius C. Wilkie Steamboat, Main Street at the Levee, (507) 454-1254 or (507) 454-6412. Take the Bluff Street exit off Highway 61 toward downtown. Turn right on Fourth Street, then left on Franklin Street to the steamboat.

From St. Louis to St. Anthony, steamboats ruled the river until the railroad made them obsolete. Along with its museum, the Julius C. Wilkie steamboat has a grand salon, which is booked for Victorian-era wedding receptions and gala balls.

While in the Area

Apart from the steamboats rolling into town, Winona is hailed as "The Stained Glass Capital of the United States." After logging acres of old-growth trees in "the big woods," Winona's nouveau riche hired the best architects in the world to design beautiful buildings to show off their riches. Many of the stained glass craftsmen who set up shop fell in love with the town and stayed.

Today, more than six different stained glass studios work out of Winona, including the country's two largest. Conway Universal Studios offers tours of their kiln firing and leading techniques at 503 Center Street; call (507) 452-9209. Ed Glubka of Conway Studios assembled an entire series of the history of the county in stained glass; these windows are on display at the Winona County Historical Society.

Winona colored glass travels around the world. Reinart's Stained Glass Studio even furnished the windows for the Vatican Chapel in Jerusalem.

To demonstrate their glass-cutting and glazing techniques, Cathedral Crafts offers occasional tours of their workshop at 730 Fifty-Fourth Avenue; call (507) 454-4079.

One of the best ways to peek at the famous stained glass is by just walking the streets. The 1889 Winona County Courthouse (Third Street and Johnson) features elaborate Victorian-style floral glass by Maybury and Son Studios. The two main banks in town, Merchants National Bank (102 East Third Street) and Winona National Bank (204 Main Street), are used to tourists wandering in and gawking at the amazing windows.

A stroll down Third Street past Merchants Bank leads to the J. R. Watkins Company (150 Liberty Street and Third Street) building from 1912, designed by Chicago architect George W. Maher. Declared "the world's finest private office building" by Laura Bergheim in her book, *An American Festival of "World's Capitals,"* the spice factory dates back more than a hundred years and is still ticking.

Next time your bath is interrupted by a solicitor, thank J. R. Watkins, who began the door-to-door sales craze by stumping spices and extracts by horse-drawn carriage across the country. Tours of the J. R. Watkins Heritage Museum and outlet store feature a view of huge stained glass windows designed by Louis J. Millet, who often worked with architect Louis Sullivan. The scene is Sugar Loaf Mountain, the 585-foot bluff hovering over the town that inspired Zeb Pike to promote this land to settlers. Call (507) 457-3300 or (507) 457-6095.

Nearly a third of Winona's inhabitants are descended from immigrants from the Kashubian region of northwestern Poland, so naturally the town's Polish Museum boasts a large collection of objects from that area. This influx of Poles resulted from Austria, Prussia, and Russia divvying up their land in 1795—Poland's loss, Minnesota's gain. Every year at the end of April, the town hits the streets for Polish Heritage Days to remember the anniversary of the 1791 Polish Constitution, to celebrate the Feast of Mary Queen of Poland, and to chomp on a few Polska Kielbasas.

Polish Cultural Institute, 102 Liberty Street, (507) 454-3431. Take the Bluff Street exit off Highway 61 toward downtown and follow the many, many signs. Summer only.

Perhaps not entirely legal in terms of zoning laws, a large houseboat community is docked on Latsch Island just outside of town. The city of Winona has allowed these boaters to weigh anchor here; after all, Huckleberry Finn lived beyond the law on his raft too. Take the Highway 43 exit and wind through town on it until the highway goes halfway over the river to Latsch Island.

Unfortunately, the Winona institution Hot Fish Shop recently closed its doors, so you'll probably end up at Jefferson's Pub & Grill (58 Center Street) near the Steamboat Museum. Even though there were two hundred speakeasies in Winona during Prohibition—more than five times as many as today—this river town still has its fair share of taverns. A favorite watering hole is Bub's Bar (pronounced "Boobs"), just off of Main Street.

Wykoff

Ed's Museum

Packrat's Paradise

Things in Wykoff are a little mixed up. The bank is a gift shop, the jail is a bed-and-breakfast, the movie theater is a community center, and the barber shop and grocery store are museums. Locals boast about the Bank Gift Haus: "Folks come all the way down from the cities to go to our store!"

Ed's Museum, however, ranks as the strangest site in town. Edwin Julius Kruger lived with his son in and above the Jack Sprat Food Store in Wykoff after his wife died in 1935. To pay the bills, Ed worked odd jobs, like running the Amazu movie theater (now the community center) and painting steeples (his harness is on display). For fifty years, he never got rid of a thing. So when he died in 1989, he left everything to the town as long as his Jack Sprat store would be turned into a museum, Ed's Museum.

Luckily, Ester Evers and Cathy Mulhern, the museum "curators" had a knack for cleaning, and they finally opened the museum after lugging six truckloads of garbage to the dump. As tour guide Donald Eickhoff says, "He never threw anything away. Nothing! Absolutely nothing! We even have all his Social Security envelopes. He had about four television sets; when one didn't work, he'd look at another."

Skeptics like the teenage clerk at the town pump slander Ed's Museum, saying, "There's just a bunch of junk!" Maybe, but to some the collection can be construed as an anthropological gold mine with every artifact of this man's life. "We don't have anything in here that isn't Ed's," according to Donald Eickhoff. Relics range from a 1920s icebox to a hand-crank washing machine and an old player piano. "He'd sit for hours and pump the pedals to play the piano."

Seems normal enough, but then there are cereal boxes with holes in the back where the mice ate everything inside; a banana tarantula spider skeleton secured in a baby food jar; and boxes of candy dried out

Ed Kruger collected everything he got his hands on during his entire life. The wall next to his piano is covered with photos of movie stars Ed never met, though he always wanted to.

from the Jack Sprat grocery store days. Ed even saved his twenty-five gallstones.

"Olde tyme" attitudes are prevalent in the section dedicated to outhouse humor. "The only man in Washington who really knows what he's doing" (he's on the toilet), reads one comic. Ed has written "Sioux Indians Chief Dewey Beard 97 in 1955 Chief's squaw heap good-Ugh!" under a photo of his visit to Cedar Lodge in the Badlands, where he is shown putting on an Indian headdress.

"Ed never made a whole lot of money, but he was a character, I tell ya!" says Eickhoff as he shows old photos of Ed dressed up with a false mustache and another with a huge parka in the store. "It was so dang cold in there, he didn't have money to heat it, so he usually wore an overcoat."

Ed apparently didn't dress very well either. "The women of Wykoff made it a habit to buy Ed new clothes every Christmastime. They thought Ed appreciated it. Then after Ed died, they found the presents—years' worth of shirts and slacks—in their original wrapping, unopened."

A journey down the rickety steps to the basement reveals stacks of every magazine Ed ever subscribed to: *Good Old Days, Modern Scream, Lutheran Witness*. Notice the secret latch on the basement door, which recalls the days when the building used to be a speakeasy and which landed it on the National Register of Historic Places.

A look around the now well-kept basement shows Ed's obsession with cats. Eickhoff explains, "He loved cats. Here's some laxatives for his cats, and those are disposable cat boxes. The last cat he had, Sammy, he took to the vet to be put to sleep. He brought it home in a plastic bag and put it in a box over ten years ago. We found the box in this basement sitting on top of a pile of dirt." He sniffs the box, "Yup, Sammy's still in there."

If that's not enough for you, the town is thinking of adding a section in back of the museum. "We have a whole second floor with Ed's stuff that we haven't touched."

The curators have already added on "The Wykoff Schools Museum," since they couldn't bear to throw away the old uniforms, desks, library cards, and yearbooks when the school closed. Eickhoff is quick to point out the old school photos: "There were more than twenty Eickhoffs in the phone book. At one point, everyone in town was related."

This new wing of the museum is located in the old barber shop, which up until recently was used by Ed to stash more junk.

Ed's Museum, c/o Bank Gift Haus, 105 Gold Street, (507) 352-4205. From I-90, take the exit onto Highway 16 at Dexter (look for the windmill). Drive twenty-two miles to Highway 80, then turn left into Wykoff. Ed's is on the right side. Weekends only.

While in the Area

Why not spend the night behind bars at the Historic Wykoff Jail Haus B & B from 1913? Wykoff has kept the cell armed with iron bars and

Other jailhouse B & Bs in the state may be more exotic, but the Wykoff Jail Haus from 1913 has kept the old bars inside and featured a mock trial and hanging at its grand opening.

bunk beds, and has even added black-and-white striped sheets and curtains. When it was opened, locals staged a trial and mock hanging to make folks feel at home. The Historic Wykoff Jail Haus B & B has four beds, two of which are bunk beds in the cell. Call (507) 325-4205.

If the Wykoff Jail is full, inmates can hole up in the Jailhouse Historic Inn in nearby Preston. A whirlpool has been added to the 1869 Fillmore County Jail to make the formal Italianate building even more plush. Even so, "The Cell Block" room is still available with "original decor" for those who can't resist life behind bars. Jailhouse Historic Inn, 109 Houston Street Northwest, Preston, (507) 765-2558.

Minnesota Events

The icehouse *Fish-scovery* blasts off in search of orbiting walleyes during the annual Fish House Parade in downtown Aitkin.

Aitkin

Fish House Parade

Claiming the unusual title of the "Fish House Capital of the World," Aitkin sponsors the annual fish house parade down Main Street (Highway 210) at the beginning of the winter fishing season. Minnesota has nearly ninety thousand licensed ice shacks, and every year the cavalcade grows with ever more bizarre and interesting designs.

Although many lakes dot the landscape around Aitkin, most fish houses head for Minnesota's premier walleye lake: Mille Lacs. More than five thousand ice shacks a year are carried onto the enormous lake, usually gathered around fishing hot spots. Summer boat landings double as entrances to ice roads that crisscross the lake in the winter.

Fish House Parade, Main Street, (218) 927-2316. Held annually on the Friday after Thanksgiving.

Austin

Spam Town, U.S.A., Festival

The music of Spam wafts across East Side Lake on the edge of Austin, where Hormel's annual corporate picnic has become the town get-together. The Spamettes sing "Spam Is a Many-Flavored Thing" in three-part harmony as spectators relish their Spam coney dogs and Spam tacos. Although locals profess their love of Spiced-Ham, they aren't afraid to laugh at the Spam phenomenon.

The Spamettes recklessly appropriate Top 40 songs, replacing the choruses with "Spam." Monty Python may have sung, "Spam, Spam, Spam, Spam Wonderful Spam!" but did they ever change the Village People's "Y.M.C.A." to "S.P.A.M." and get hundreds to sing along, making the letters with their bodies? As the Spamettes break into "In the Food," rather than "In the Mood," it's time to check out the food court, where even Godfather's has a special Spam pizza for the festival.

The kids, on the other hand, are more concerned with the pork-related amusement park. The Spam "Magic" Mountain is the favorite, with a big pile of Spam cans and prizes in only a few of them. The Spam Suds Crawl involves climbing up a soaped-down slide and trying to put the Spam can in a hole. The least-favorite, however, is the Spam Gelatin Jump: "It's basically all the white stuff around Spam in a big vat. You stick your arms in and pull out a golf ball for a prize," says the attendant.

Usually, the beautiful blue-and-yellow Spambelle mini-paddleboat from 1956 is one of the star attractions, but it sank the previous night on live TV. A fairgoer explains, "They had to pull it out with a crane. I guess the captain ate too much Spam!"

It's possible, considering that the miracle meat is on sale for only a buck a can at this Spam Jamboree. "This is a great deal because if you go to a SuperAmerica, a can of Spam will cost upwards of $1.60 each!" says the salesman, who already had his own bag full.

To inaugurate the annual Spam Jamboree, Hormel's official mini-Spambelle Paddleboat putts across East Side Lake to the docks of the festival.

One year, massive quantities of Spam were allocated to the most talented sculptors in town to carve temporary statues out of everyone's favorite spiced ham. Who knows, maybe even Michelangelo made models in pork before cementing his ideas in marble? Rodin's *The Thinker* was the favorite of the show.

Unfortunately for the artistically inclined tourists, Spam sculptures turned out to be a one-time event. "All that food would be better put to use to feed the hungry," says Hormel representative Mary Harris. "Besides, it just gets kind of gross."

Spam Jam, East Side Lake, (507) 437-5345. Take exit 180A from I-90 on the east side of Austin and look for the Spam cans by the lake. Held every Fourth of July weekend.

Blackduck

Duck Days

When Bemidji was basking in the limelight from articles in *Life* and the *New York Times* about their 1937 Winter Carnival, little Blackduck thought they would jump on the bandwagon with (what else?) a huge portable black duck that Paul Bunyan hunted. Ranger

The original black duck greeted visitors at the wayside park along Highway 71 until a nearby creamery burned down, endangering the town symbol. The flammable duck was hastily moved to safety on Main Street, next to the fire station and the Do Duck Inn.

P. J. St. Amant built the huge bird at Camp Ribideau, putting it on sled runners so the Blackduck queen could ride the duck through town. As a bonus, Paul Bunyan's gigantic three-barreled musket was placed on the float and actually fired.

The duck rode in front of Babe the Blue Ox at the 1938 Bemidji Winter Carnival, then went south on tour to the prestigious St. Paul Winter Carnival. Dayton's department store featured the duck in its store window for a week before the festivities, and the *St. Paul Pioneer Press* encouraged spectators to see the beast that would be big enough to feed 1,862 people duck soup. When it came time for the much-awaited parade, the black duck nearly got stuck in the auditorium doors and had to exit the main entrance backward.

The duck's touring days have been replaced by the annual "Duck Days" each July. According to the Blackduck town brochure, one of the favorite activities is "Jail and Bail." "Have one of your favorite people jailed," the brochure recommends, "and see how they'll get out."

Duck Days, (218) 835-4669 or 1-800-323-2975. Held in late July.

Crosslake

Drive-In Church

Members of the Crosslake Evangelical Lutheran Church were tired of putting on their Sunday best every week, so during the summer months, Reverend Mark Anderson now gathers his congregation at a field just outside of town to preach the word—only all the believers are safely behind the windshields of their cars.

With drive-in restaurants, theaters, and banks dotting the landscape, this Lutheran church decided in 1971 to extend the sacrament to the motoring set. Up to five hundred people roll into the field and are escorted to their parking spots by men in orange vests who pass out the programs for the day's prayer. At 10:00 A.M., the service begins with a chorus of horns honking hallelujah. "Some of you have your lights on," warns Pastor Mark.

Kids hop out of the cars and gather at a picnic table at the edge of the field for Sunday school. Deer and fox sometimes wander into the meadow, unaware that people are perched behind their steering wheels praying. When a curious bear strolled into the congregation a few years ago, all the children scurried back to the safety of their respective cars.

With the radio tuned to 93.1 FM, the reverend's voice comes in loud and clear over the airwaves. No need for special aids for the hard of hearing—just crank the volume. Worshippers don't worry about crooning hymns out of tune since little can be heard outside their cars. They can even munch on donuts without fearing the wrath of the reverend; actually the good-natured pastor often picks up sweet rolls for the congregation as another incentive to drive in to praise the Lord.

The congregation only ventures out of their cars for Communion, to partake in the communal coffeepot, and to visit the line of port-o-potties on the edge of the parking lot.

Once a summer, during the "Blessing of the Animals," pets run around the sanctuary/parking lot and Pastor Mark calls upon the

Almighty to purify our furry friends. The idea has been so successful that he now sanctifies the entire parking lot during Classic Car Sunday, hoping to make mechanics obsolete.

"I suppose you think we're weird," he chuckles, "but people love coming outside here to worship in the beautiful surroundings." License plates from as far away as Texas, Florida, and Virginia drive up for the unusual ceremony.

At the climax of the sermon, drivers honk their amens, then rev their engines to be the first out of the parking lot. "Once they've had their coffee and donuts," says Pastor Mark, "they get going fast."

Crosslake Evangelical Lutheran Drive-In Church, (218) 692-3682. From Brainerd, take Highway 210 northeast to Crosby, turn north on Highway 6 and drive about twelve miles to County Road 36. Turn left and drive about five miles into town. The service is held across from the community center every Sunday in the summer at 10:00 A.M.

Honk if you love Jesus! Pastor Mark Anderson calls his congregation to his weekly service and preaches from his A-frame altar to the choir in their cars.

Cuyuna

Woodtick Races

"If you can't beat 'em, race 'em!" should be the motto of tiny Cuyuna, near Crosby, which hosts the annual and "nationally famous" Woodtick Races in mid-June. When you roll into town, look for the truck selling the beer paraphernalia with T-shirts like "King of Rears: Butt-weiser." Be careful not to broadside the line of Harleys, and pull in at the only store/bar in town: the Woodtick Inn. "Racing Steeds Available on Premises," read the signs, where for a whopping dollar bill you can buy a tick from a teenager in a seed cap. He describes his harvesting method: "Me and a buddy went running out in the woods near Emily in swim trunks."

"That's disgusting," yells a woman impatiently waiting in line for a tick.

A large bearded man with a pair of beers in his hands comes to his defense, "Hey, he's making a living!"

"Yeah!" rebuts the teen self-righteously, continuing to make change for the growing line of shoppers.

If you choose to reap your own ticks, take a little girl's advice: "My daddy just lied in the tall grass."

More than 150 eager jockeys roam around "the track"—the parking lot next to the Woodtick Inn—with their beloved woodticks in covered Dixie cups strapped around their necks with nametags like "Flash" and "Cuyuna's Pride." Rules are strict, however, as a brochure warns, "Cheating will not be tolerated—a certified woodtick veterinarian will be on-site to test the ticks for steroids!"

At 12:30 P.M., all jockeys are called to the track to establish the rules; at 1:00 P.M. sharp the races begin. Two ticks are coaxed into the center of a ring and the first to scurry to the edge wins. When asked about a grand prize, one of the female judges replies, astonished, "Grand prize?" Then points to her friend and says, "Well, you can have *her!*"

At the end of the races, the exhausted participants retire to the Woodtick Inn to have a cold one; all that excitement and coaxing bugs builds a thirst. The inside of the inn is lined with old hubcaps sprouting dangling limbs, making them appear to be woodticks. I asked the bartender if there is a jockey hall of fame. "Hall of Fame? What are you, crazy? They're just woodticks!"

Woodtick Races. Call (218) 546-5313. From Brainerd, go northeast on Highway 210 to Crosby. Drive through town to County Road 1 and turn left to Cuyuna. Races are held each July next to the Woodtick Inn.

Deer River

Wild Rice Festival

The true Minnesota staple grows on many of the more than fifteen thousand lakes across the state. Paddle a canoe into the tall grass, bend the stalks over the side, and beat it. Black seeds pile up between the gunwales on the bottom of the boat, meaning an abundant harvest and plenty of wild rice hotdish, with the addition of cream of mushroom soup, of course.

On the edge of the Leech Lake Indian Reservation, the town of Deer River boils up this aquatic grass in huge kettles during its annual Wild Rice Festival, held in mid-July. While people munch on the rice, a chainsaw-carving competition roars nearby for dinnertime amusement.

Sometimes at special occasions inside the Leech Lake Indian Reservation, "Wild Game Buffets" will be laid out where guests can eat for free, since hunters can't sell their take. If you're lucky enough to be a guest, eat your way through the state as a plethora of Minnesota's critters—from deer to wild turkey, bear to moose—can please your palate.

Wild Rice Festival, (218) 246-8195. From Grand Rapids, take Highway 2 northwest thirteen miles to Deer River. The annual festival is held each July in downtown Deer River.

293

Falcon Heights

Minnesota State Fair

Nothing is more of a microcosm of the state than the "Big Minnesota Get-Together." Everyone goes for a different reason: farmers bring their cows, dancers go to polka, politicians press the flesh, and race car drivers blast their twelve-cylinder double overhead cam hemis around endless laps.

Some visitors wouldn't miss the latest crop-art designs of corn, soybeans, and wheat laid out to portray George Washington, the Backstreet Boys, and even Jesse Ventura. Others just have to drop a penny into the antique flip photo machines, showing movies like "Striptease," in which a secretary seduces her boss by showing some stocking and then whacks him upside the head for being fresh.

Where else can you munch on a pork chop on a stick and gasp at the state's fattest hog? Or load up on all-you-can-drink milk for fifty cents and then watch a dog get spayed?

On Machinery Hill, booths try to lure you in with a Dixie cup of ice water, hoping you'll invest in a new water heater or a John Deere combine. Everything's mechanical—chainsaws have even chiseled away all the dead elms into State Fair staples: corncobs and pronto pups.

Carnies on the Midway bellow to the crowd to see the Wall of Death, to enter the once-ubiquitous freak shows, and to ride the roller coasters, which you hope have been checked for loose bolts before the thrills and spills.

In the Agricultural Building, a man with a microphone headset chatters like an auctioneer as he slices and dices, then reveals a rutabaga flower. "Look, you can wear it as a corsage!" he announces. Ronco is still the leader in kitchen gizmos.

The State Fair is the showpiece for the entire state. Where radio DJs desperately blast AC/DC to annoyed pedestrians (and a few nostalgic metalheads) and well-bred public radio listeners chuckle at another of

To many fairgoers, the State Fair is all about eating anything on a stick, but others prefer to visit one of the classic lunch counters or dining halls for a relaxing sit-down meal.

Garrison Keillor's shy-person jokes. Where you can plug a nickel into the 1940s arcade game Atomic Bomber and pretend to fly the Enola Gay for the Stars-n-Stripes. Where Princess Kay of the Milky Way climbs into a refrigerated room and has her head carved in an enormous chunk of butter. The State Fair is Minnesota, warts and all.

Minnesota State Fair, 1265 Snelling Avenue North, (651) 642-2200. From I-94 take the Snelling Avenue (Highway 51) exit north two miles. The fairgrounds are on the left. The fair is held for ten days, ending on Labor Day.

La Crescent

King Apple Grand Parade

J ohn S. Harris was Minnesota's Johnny Appleseed. Critics scoffed at his attempts to plant apple groves in this harsh northern climate,

La Crescent was named after the crescent moon symbol, often seen on flags of Muslim nations, to rival La Crosse across the river—even though La Crosse wasn't named after "the Cross." This Wisconsin neighbor is a mecca for beer, as shown by the World's Largest Six Pack: six silos filled with enough Old Style for 22,200 barrels of beer, or 7,340,950 cans.

but he did it anyway. In 1872, his crops were almost entirely wiped out by an early freeze, but headstrong Johnny Harris was out the next spring sowing seeds. A dozen years later, when the trees began to bear fruit, a vicious cold snap ruined his crops and destroyed much of his apple orchard. Not one to be proved wrong, Harris stubbornly dispersed his seeds and eventually put La Crescent in the history books as the "Apple Capital of the World."

Thanks to Harris's bullheaded determination, La Crescent has more than a thousand acres of apple trees with sixty-five different varieties of apples. Even the Minnesota State Horticultural Society has its roots here.

Every year during the third weekend of September, apples are everywhere in La Crescent: Apple Annie Night at the American Legion, the Applefest Demolition Derby, the Applefest run or walk, the Apple Cobbler Golf Open, and, of course, the Johnny Appleseed Tent, where singers croon about the glories of apples. During the excitement of Applefest, lovers can slink away to smooch by following the apples under the road signs for a romantic drive along Apple Blossom Scenic Drive. The King Apple Grand Parade tops off the event, with the crowned fruited royalty waving from their apple float on Main Street.

King Apple Grand Parade, Main Street, (507) 895-2800. From I-90, turn south on Highway 61 into La Crescent. Third weekend in September.

Luverne

Buffalo Days

Just north of Luverne, a buffalo herd roams Blue Mounds State Park, producing little prizes for the town's June festival. Underneath rock climbers scaling a ninety-foot cliff, locals trudge through the thick virgin prairie of the glacial mounds, gathering dried buffalo pies, just like Native Americans used to do. Collectors have found a much more creative use for bison excrement than simply starting campfires for cooking interestingly flavored food.

Three teams are lined up and given three chips each. "These are real authentic dried buffalo chips from the herd of buffalo at Blue Mounds State Park," brags the Luverne brochure. An official "Chip Inspector" makes the rounds with a ruler to make sure the chips are regulation size. The "Buffalo Chips Throwing Contest" begins as contestants try to land the dried dung in toilets ten and fifteen feet away. Winners and losers of this scatological discus toss and then line up for another gift from the prairie: buffalo burgers.

Buffalo Days, downtown Luverne, (507) 283-4061. From I-90, take the Luverne exit north into town. First weekend in June.

Blue Mounds State Park. Continue through Luverne on Highway 75 and turn right on County Road 20 into the park. Also go to the Prairie School–style interpretive center off of Highway 8, where author Frederick Manfred once lived. Call (507) 283-4548 or (507) 283-4892.

Minneapolis

Aquatennial Milk Carton Boat Races

The Aquatennial, the annual summer hoopla of the City of Lakes, features such events as the Torchlight Parade, where you can see marching bands, floats, and celebrities galore. In spite of the sophistication of the state's largest metropolis, Minneapolis lets go of its pretensions during this one week of the year, as illustrated by the goofy Milk Carton Boat Races.

Contestants needn't guzzle all that milk: a local dairy generously donates thousands of empty cartons for the tippy vessels. Creativity abounds as builders construct everything from enormous cow catamarans to bright yellow school bus skiffs. Some of these homemade ships hold up to fifteen people, but a diligent lifeguard is on watch in case the boats turn turtle.

Milk Carton Races. East side of Lake Nokomis, (612) 331-8371. From I-35W, take the Forty-Sixth Avenue exit east, turn right at Cedar Avenue and then left on Minnehaha Parkway. Lake Nokomis is on the south side of the road. Mid-July.

A red, white, and blue steamboat makes the finals at the Milk Carton Boat Races on Lake Nokomis. These multipassenger vessels race to the finish line in various heats and, incredibly, rarely tip over.

Looking like a float in a parade, Ripper the Friendly Shark putts down Lyndale Avenue in Minneapolis. Creator Tom Kennedy drove his landshark all the way from Houston, Texas, where the National Art Car Museum is located.

Minneapolis

Art Car Parade

In a reaction to Detroit's ho-hum automobile designs, artists have taken this cornerstone of the American dream as their own canvas. Springs, cameras, corks, bones, maps, and even grass have been glued to cars in this attack on conformity.

In 1998, an especially unusual art car showed up at the south Minneapolis event, the "Jerungdu Kale Farm Truck," with a trailer hauling a musical band of men and women dressed only in kale. When the hot sun started wilting their green clothes, the Minneapolis police nearly stepped in to make an arrest for public nudity.

An easy comparison can be made between these moveable art pieces and festival floats, but these altered automobiles usually run year-round. Unlike dragsters, most art cars are old jalopies driven by their final owners. Once artists have spent months altering their autos, however, a seven-hundred-dollar engine rebuild isn't so bad compared to seeing their labor of love in the trash compacter.

It's a duty, once in the life of any art car owner, to venture to the ultimate art car attraction, Car Henge in Alliance, Nebraska. Art professor Ruthann Godollei was so moved by her trip to this masterpiece in the middle of the stark prairie that she decided to stage a winter version of the art car parade on the frozen expanse of Lake Minnetonka. Minnesota art cars slipped and slid around on the frozen lake, much to the bewilderment of the ice fishermen. Not surprisingly, few spectators braved the windchill, but at least a short film, "Art Cars on Ice," was made so the artists could have bragging rights when it was shown at the summer event.

Art Car Parade, Intermedia Arts, 2822 Lyndale Avenue South, (612) 871-4444. From I-94, take the Lyndale exit south just past Twenty-Eighth Avenue. Intermedia Arts is on the right. Mid-August.

Northfield

Defeat of Jesse James Days

J esse James, Bob Younger, and Charlie Pitts were quietly eating breakfast in a Northfield diner on September 7, 1876. They'd already held
up banks from Kentucky to Texas, so Minnesota seemed like a good
backwater for continuing their spree.

While they finished their bacon and eggs, Frank James, two Younger
brothers, and a couple of other hoodlums stormed the town to create
a diversion. The three diners raced across the street into the First
National Bank and demanded that the safe be opened. Banker Joseph
Lee Heywood played a trick on the gangsters while they shoved their
guns into his face. He told them stone-faced that it was impossible to
open the huge steel safe, declining to divulge that the door was always
wide open during regular banking hours. The little joke would be his
last, however, as Jesse James shot him in cold blood. The bank teller
had held up the three gangsters long enough, however, for young medical student Henry Wheeler to open fire on the outlaws.

With bullets flying overhead, the James-Younger gang realized the
holdup had gone sour and they made a break for it. Residents of Northfield formed a posse and ran them out of town. Charlie Pitts was chased
down and shot, and the three Younger brothers were thrown into Stillwater Prison for twenty-five years. One of the thieves, Clel Miller, lay
dead in the street and was later carefully dissected by medical students.

Ironically, the only two not captured or killed in the seven-minute
melee were Jesse and Frank James. The brothers hid out in Dakota territory for three years, then started up their outlaw ways again. Jesse
James was finally gunned down six years later in Missouri.

Some historians claim the Northfield holdup was the last battle of the
Civil War, since two despised Northerners, former Union generals Butler
and Ames, owned the bank. The James-Younger gang presumably
wanted to win one final battle for the South. According to *Historic*

Festivals by George Cantor, "The Northfield raid . . . signaled a clear warning about the hazards of robbing banks in Minnesota." The bank Jesse James tried to hold up is now a museum.

Northfield stages a shoot-'em-up reenactment every day during what was once called "Jesse James Days." To avoid condoning his behavior, the name of the festival has been changed to "The Defeat of Jesse James Days"—even though the James brothers escaped.

Defeat of Jesse James Days, downtown Northfield, 1-800-658-2548. From I-35, take Highway 19 east into Northfield. Held the weekend after Labor Day.

Pequot Lakes

Beanhole Days

"It's been said that the scent alone will stop a car," according to the town brochure about the huge cauldrons with 150 gallons of "Pequot Lakes Boston Baked Beans."

Legend says that pioneers were in the midst of cooking supper when they heard that a group of Indians was about to attack. They quickly buried their pots of beans and camouflaged them with underbrush. When they came back, the beans were tastier than ever, and Pequot Lakes was thereafter known as the "Beanhole Capital of the World."

Ever since the logging camps of 1935, fire pits have been dug, lined with rocks, and filled with beans that are cooked for days in anticipation of the annual rendezvous. In 1938, five hundred people showed up to eat beans and participate in the annual tug-of-war between farmers and businessmen. Needless to say, the farmers continually clean house.

Although there's no coronation of a Beanhole Queen, a King Bean is crowned each year and given the solemn responsibility of serving the first batch of beans.

In 1995, local headlines blared, "Pequot Police Chief Suspects Kettle Heist," when festival organizers forgot where they left the cooking cauldrons from the year before. The six large pots—named Sven, Ole, Lena, Big Bertha, Baby Olga, and Thor—were soon found and the fairgoers got their beans.

Beanhole Days, downtown Pequot Lakes, (218) 568-8521. Drive thirty minutes north of Brainerd on Highway 371; the festival is in the park on the right side of the road. Held on the Fourth of July.

Red Wing

Prairie Island Powwow

The largest island on the Mississippi hosts one of the most important powwows in the state just after the Fourth of July weekend. Many tourists make a beeline for the Treasure Island Casino next door, but the real excitement is outside in the parking lot. Representatives from tribes all around the area dance in their kaleidoscopic outfits to the thumping sacred drums, delighting the crowd. Chomp on some fresh fry bread, maybe with a little venison, and enjoy the show.

Prairie Island Powwow, (651) 385-5934. From the Twin Cities, go southeast on Highway 61 (Highway 10). After Hastings, veer left on Highway 316 and follow the signs to Treasure Island Casino on the Prairie Island Indian Reservation. The powwow is next to the casino. Early July.

St. Paul

Winter Carnival

Minnesota winters are all about being tough enough. When some-one decides to move to warmer climes, the inevitable response is, "So you can't hack it, eh?" A sort of mass delirium keeps the state populated during these cold months, since no one wants to show that the cold actually gets to them.

When a highbrow New York journalist visited Minnesota's capital in 1885 and dared to write that St. Paul was "another Siberia, unfit for human habitation," something had to be done. To show that St. Paul was actually a winter wonderland, huge bricks of ice from a nearby lake were stacked 106 feet high to make the city's first ice castle. St. Paulites took to the streets in droves to see this marvel and march in the first Winter Carnival parade. Unfortunately, the mercury plunged to -20° for the occasion; the number of frostbite cases was never reported.

St. Paul's native son F. Scott Fitzgerald wrote about this bizarre Min-nesota phenomenon in a 1920 short story called "The Ice Palace." A young woman from Georgia is engaged to a man from St. Paul, but just when she's scheduled to meet her fiancé's family, she somehow gets locked inside of the ice castle. When she finally escapes, the wedding is called off and she flees Minnesota for the southland. Obviously, she couldn't hack it.

St. Paul Winter Carnival, downtown St. Paul, (651) 297-6953. Last weekend of January to the first weekend in February.

This fake matchbook advertisement played up each festival event with a different match inside: MUSICAL JAMBOREE, CURLING BONSPIEL, MAJORETTE CONTEST, and QUEEN OF THE SNOWS BALL. Just strike the simulated match on the real sandpaper provided.

Sno-Daze in North St. Paul just wasn't the same without even a dusting of snow on the ground, so the local Jaycees built a year-round snowman. The huge Frosty (located at Highway 36 and Margaret Street) doubles as a storage shed for Christmas lights, with a secret trapdoor in the rear.

Walker

International Eelpout Festival

Every February in subzero weather, a town of icehouses forms on Leech Lake near Walker in search of the "Ugliest fish in the world," according to festival advertisements. "Eelpout," slimy, prehistoric-looking fish, are dragged from the bottom of the lake and the bizarre festivities begin.

Newspapers run goofy articles with headlines joking, "Pout-Jones Intestinal Averages." The festival culminates with a contest to see who can catch the biggest, and therefore the ugliest, eelpout.

International Eelpout Festival, on Leech Lake near Walker, (218) 547-1313. Walker is ninety minutes north of Brainerd on Highway 371, then drive out onto the lake. February.

Waterville

Bullhead Days

When fishermen would try to bring home supper from Sakatah Lake, they usually ended up with bullheads on their line. Rather than putting on thick gloves and risking the stingers of the grumpy-looking fish to get their lures back, most would simply snip the line and chuck the fish into the bushes.

Instead of turning its head in shame, Waterville took advantage of this bountiful natural resource, gathering the whole town each year for "Bullhead Days" in early June. Although no bullhead statue graces downtown yet, a "Queen Pageant" is part of the festivities—luckily, they opted against dubbing the top princess the "Bullhead Queen."

To rid the swimming areas of the stinging creatures and turn bullheads into fishes, festival organizers head down to the lake and pull out as many of the bottom feeders as possible. Heavy leather gloves help them avoid getting zapped as they rip off the skin with pliers and throw the stripped fish into a vat of sizzling oil. Hungry fairgoers line up for a sample of what locals consider a delicacy. Afterward, most diners head for the beer tent to wash back the dark meat with a cold one. "They don't taste so bad," claims one of the fish vendors. "Once you deep-fry them, you can hardly tell it's bullhead."

Bullhead Days, downtown Waterville, (507) 362-8403 or (507) 362-4609. From I-35, take Highway 60 west (not toward Faribault). Drive fifteen miles, then turn north on Highway 13 and follow your nose into town. Early June.

Whalen

Stand Still Parade

With a population of eighty-six and a main street that stretches only about a block, Whalen was too small for a blowout festival. Revelers decided to stop marching back and forth and instead stage a parade that stays put and lets the crowd do the walking. Even CBS

Across Minnesota, corn feeds and festivals, like Corn Days in Lime Springs, bring small communities together in the late summer.

stopped by to film all the floats, marching bands, and dairy queens waving to the masses from their stagnant cars.

Stand Still Parade, downtown Whalen, (507) 467-2696. From I-90, take Highway 52 southeast to Chatfield. Take Highway 30 east out of town about ten miles to Highway 250. Turn right into Lanesboro, then take Highway 16 into Whalen.

Worthington.

Great Gobbler Gallop

When Worthington found out that their claim as the Turkey Capital of the World was questioned by Cuero, Texas, it was time for a duel between the Lone Star State and the Land of 10,000 Lakes. Rather than getting bogged down in court, Worthington officials created the "Great Gobbler Gallop" to determine who had the fastest turkey, which first showers its hometown with glory and then makes a succulent Thanksgiving dinner. The winning town gets the "Traveling Trophy of Tumultuous Triumph," at least until next year.

Great Gobbler Gallop, downtown Worthington, (507) 372-2919. Take the Worthington exit off of I-90.

Bibliography

Baskas, Harriet, and Adam Woog. 1993. *Atomic Marbles and Branding Irons: A Guide to Museums, Collections, and Roadside Curiosities in Washington and Oregon*. Seattle: Sasquatch Books.

Bergheim, Laura. 1997. *An American Festival of "World Capitals": From Garlic Queens to Cherry Parades*. New York: John Wiley and Sons, Inc.

Blashfield, Jean F. 1993. *Awesome Almanac: Minnesota*. Fontana, Wisc.: B & B Publishing.

Breining, Greg. 1997. *Minnesota*. Oakland, Calif.: Compass American Guides, Fodor's Travel Publications, Inc.

Cantor, George. 1996. *Historic Festivals: A Traveler's Guide*. Detroit: Visible Ink.

Clynes, Tom. 1996. *Music Festivals from Bach to Blues: A Traveler's Guide*. Detroit: Visible Ink.

DeGroot, Barbara, and Jack El-Hai. 1995. *The Insiders' Guide to the Twin Cities*. Manteo, N.C.: Insiders' Guides.

Dickson, Paul, and Robert Skole. 1995. *The Volvo Guide to Halls of Fame: The Traveler's Handbook of North America's Most Inspiring and Entertaining Attractions*. Washington, D.C.: Living Planet Press.

Dos Passos, John. *Nineteen Nineteen*. 1937. Boston: Houghton Mifflin.

Dregni, Michael, ed. 1999. *Minnesota Days: Our Heritage in Stories, Art, and Photos*. Stillwater, Minn.: Voyageur Press.

Frost, Robert. 1946. *The Poems of Robert Frost*. New York: Random House.

Gauper, Beth. 1996. *Midwest Weekends: Memorable Getaways in the Upper Midwest*. Kansas City, Mo.: Andrews & McMeel.

Gurvis, Sandra. 1998. *America's Strangest Museums: A Traveler's Guide to the Most Unusual and Eccentric Collections*. Toronto: Citadel Press.

Harris, Moira. 1992. *Monumental Minnesota: A Guide to Outdoor Sculpture*. St. Paul: Pogo Press.

Hauck, Dennis William. 1996. *National Directory of Haunted Places*. New York: Penguin.

Kimball, Joe. 1985. *Secrets of the Congdon Mansion*. Minneapolis: JayKay Pub. Inc.

Lavenda, Robert H. 1997. *Corn Fests and Water Carnivals: Celebrating Community in Minnesota*. Washington, D.C.: Smithsonian Institution Press.

Lee, Carvel. 1990. *Thirty-Six One-Day Discovery Tours*. Minneapolis: Nodin Press.

Lonto, Jeff. 1998. *Legend of the Brewery: A Brief History of the Minneapolis Brewing Heritage*. Minneapolis: Studio Z-7 Publishing.

Maccabee, Paul. 1995. *John Dillinger Slept Here: A Crooks' Tour of Crime and Corruption in St. Paul, 1920–1936*. St. Paul: Minnesota Historical Society Press.

MacDougall, Curtis D. 1958. *Hoaxes*. New York: Dover.

Margolies, John. 1998. *Fun along the Road: American Tourist Attractions*. Boston: Bulfinch Press.

Marling, Karal Ann. 1990. *Blue Ribbon: A Social and Pictorial History of the Minnesota State Fair*. St. Paul: Minnesota Historical Society Press.

———. 1984. *The Colossus of Roads: Myth and Symbol along the American Highway*. Minneapolis: University of Minnesota Press.

Millett, Larry. 1992. *Lost Twin Cities*. St. Paul: Minnesota Historical Society Press.

Norman, Scott, and Michael Norman. 1985. *Haunted Heartland*. New York: Warner Books.

O'Reilly, Jane H. 1998. *Quick Escapes: Minneapolis/St. Paul*. Old Saybrook, Conn.: Globe Pequot Press.

Rubin, Saul. 1997. *Offbeat Museums: The Collections and Curators of America's Most Unusual Museums*. Santa Monica, Calif.: Santa Monica Press.

Sandburg, Carl. 1936. *The People, Yes*. New York: Harcourt, Brace.

Sergeant, John. 1976. *Frank Lloyd Wright's Usonian Houses: The Case for Organic Architecture*. New York: Whitney Library of Design.

Shepard, John. 1989. *Minnesota: Off the Beaten Path*. Chester, Conn.: Globe Pequot Press.

Simonowicz, Nina. 1999. *Nina's North Shore Guide*. Minneapolis: University of Minnesota Press.

Stein, Gordon, and Marie MacNee. 1995. *Hoaxes: Dupes, Dodges, and Other Dastardly Deceptions*. Detroit: Visible Ink.

Stelling, Lucille Johnsen. 1988. *Frommer's Guide to Minneapolis and St. Paul*. New York: Simon and Schuster.

Wilkins, Mike, Ken Smith, and Doug Kirby. 1992. *The New Roadside America*. New York: Simon and Schuster.

Wilson, Blanche Nichols. 1950. *Minnetonka Story.* Minneapolis: Ross and Haines Inc.

Winter, Laurel. 1990. *Minnesota Trivia.* Nashville, Tenn.: Rutledge Hill Press.

W.P.A. 1941. *The W.P.A. Guide to the Minnesota Arrowhead Country.* St. Paul: Minnesota Historical Society Press.

Permissions for Photographs

The University of Minnesota Press is grateful to these people and institutions for permission to reproduce the photographs on the pages indicated. The name of the photographer, if known, is given in parentheses. Most of the other photographs in the book were taken by the author.

Aitkin Independent Age: 282

Bakken Museum: 134

Down in History Tours: 219

El Dorado Conquistador Museum: 212

Ruthann Godollei (photographer): 302

Minnesota Historical Society: 21, 52 (Roger Kennedy), 111 (Gjelhaug), 117, 127, 129 (C. Edwards Studio), 178, 215, 233 (Gordon Ray), 244 *(Minneapolis Tribune)*

Roseau County Historical Society: 202

Index

ERIC DREGNI was born in the shadow of the World's Largest Six-Pack in La Crosse, Wisconsin (but immediately defected over the border into Minnesota). He has written *Ads That Put America on Wheels* and three books on motor scooters. He also plays in the mock-rock trio Vinnie & the Stardüsters.